John R. Sweney, William J. Kirkpatrick, Charles H. Yatman

Temple Songs

John R. Sweney, William J. Kirkpatrick, Charles H. Yatman

Temple Songs

ISBN/EAN: 9783337815424

Printed in Europe, USA, Canada, Australia, Japan

Cover: Foto ©Lupo / pixelio.de

More available books at **www.hansebooks.com**

TEMPLE SONGS

(SEASIDE EDITION.)

SELECTED BY

CHARLES H. YATMAN.

MUSICAL EDITORS:

JNO. R. SWENEY AND WM. J. KIRKPATRICK.

PHILADELPHIA:
Published by JOHN J. HOOD, 1018 Arch St.

Temple · Songs

Hide Thou Me.

FANNY J. CROSBY.   "Thou art my hiding place."—Ps. xxxii. 7.   ROBERT LOWRY. By per.

1. In thy cleft, O Rock of a-ges, Hide thou me; When the fitful tempest ra-ges, Hide thou me; Where no mortal arm can sev-er From my heart thy love forev-er, Hide me, O thou Rock of a-ges, Safe in thee.
2. From the snare of sinful pleasure, Hide thou me; Thou, my soul's eternal trea-sure, Hide thou me; When the world its power is wielding, And my heart is almost yielding, Hide me, O thou Rock of a-ges, Safe in thee.
3. In the lonely night of sorrow, Hide thou me; Till in glory dawns the mor-row, Hide thou me; In the sight of Jordan's bil-low, Let thy bo-som be my pillow; Hide me, O thou Rock of a-ges, Safe in thee.

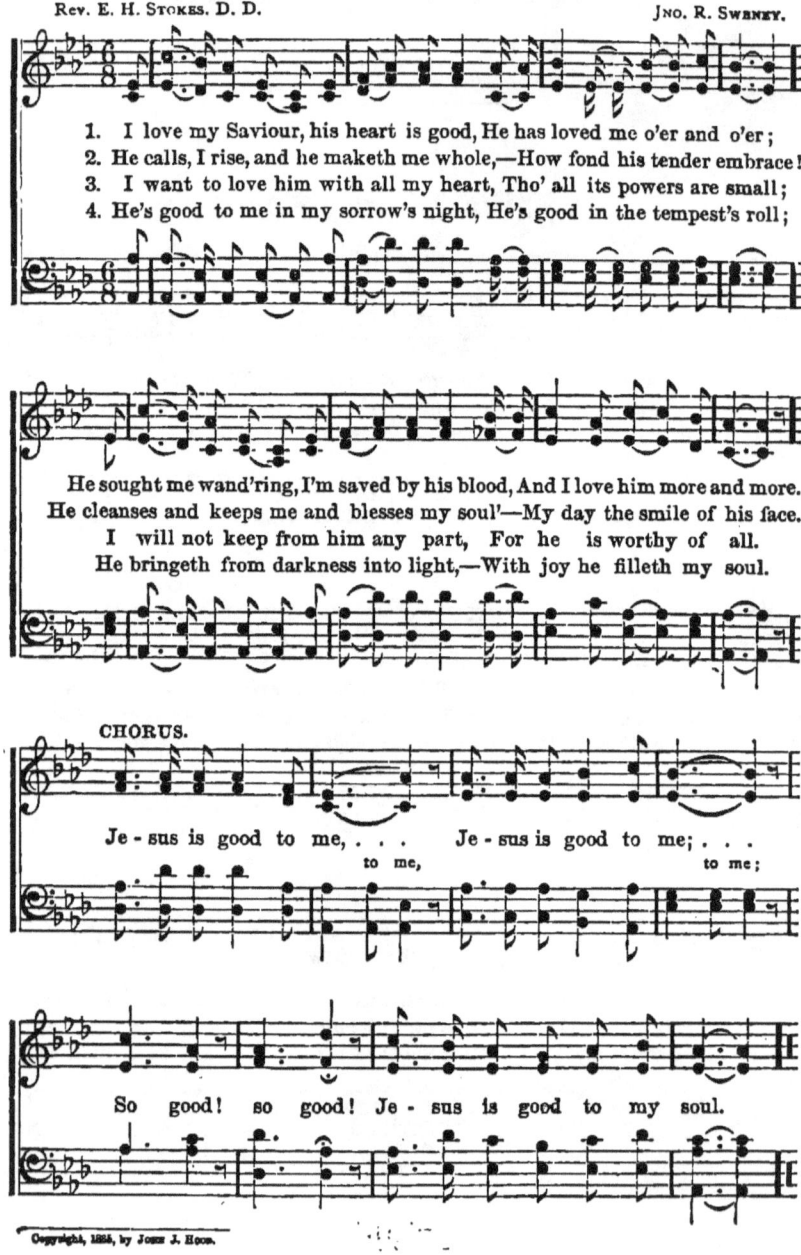

Abiding.

Rev. E. H. Stokes, D. D. Jno. R. Sweney.

1. My soul for light and love had earnest longings, Oh, how it longed for fellowship divine! I sought it here and there, I sought it ev'rywhere, At last thro' faith, the ho-ly boon was mine.
2. Oh, how enrich-ing is this sacred treasure! En-riching to this soul, this soul of mine; There's nothing anywhere Can with this love compare, And I henceforth, for-ev-er, Lord, am thine.
3. Oh, yes, I rest, how blessed is the rest-ing! I rest to-day, I'm resting all the time. "Come," echoes thro' the air, "Come," and the resting share, And Je-sus will be yours as he is mine.

CHORUS.

I'm a-bid-ing, gracious Sa-viour, I'm a-bid-ing in thy precious love to-day; I'm a-bid-ing, yes, a-bid-ing In thy love, thy precious love, to-day.

Copyright 1882, by John J. Hood.

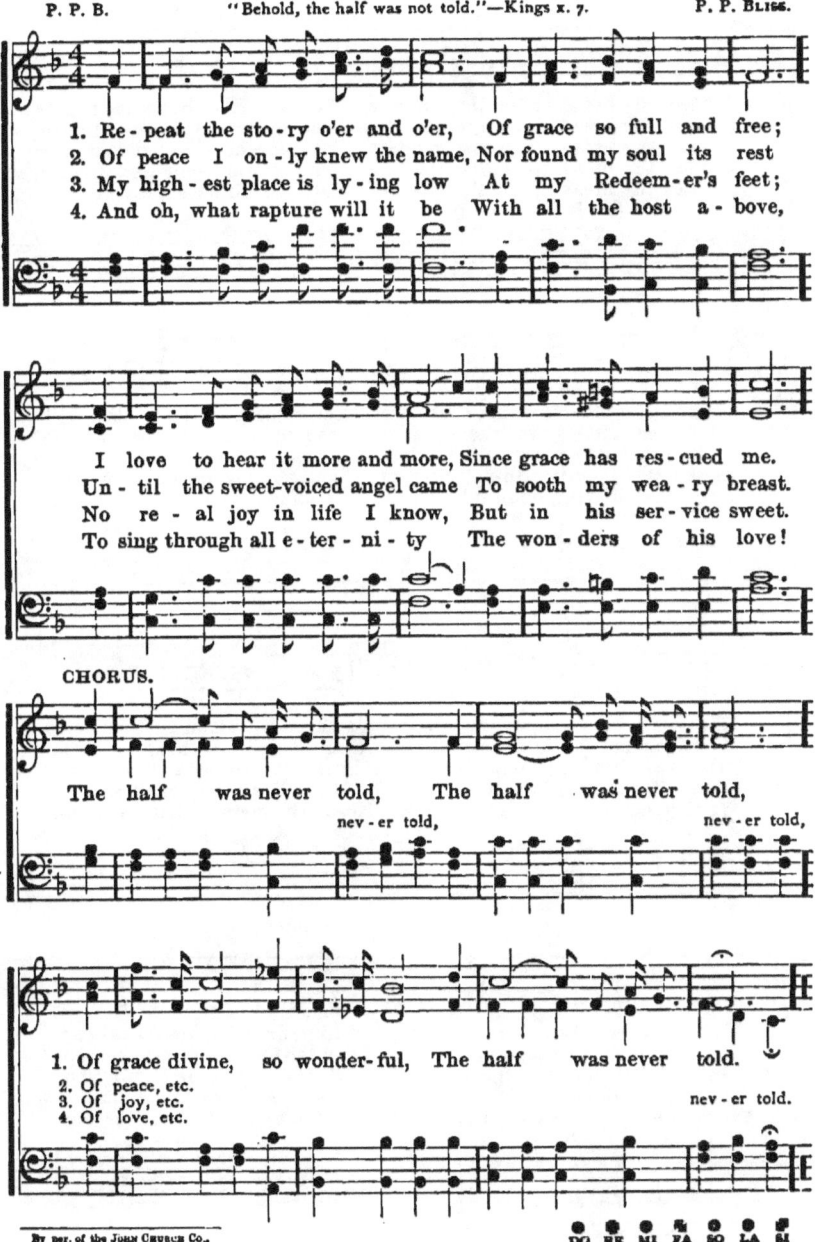

Praise to Thee, Mighty One.

Mrs. R. N. Turner. Wm. J. Kirkpatrick.

1. Praise to thee, Mighty One, Throned in the sky, Heav'n and earth worship thee
2. Author of every good, King o-ver all, Un-to thy ho-ly name
3. Vast as thy pow'r and strength, Thy wondrous love; Drawing each heart and voice
4. Praise to thee, Mighty One! From earth and heaven, Praise to thee, Holy One!

Lord God on high! Holy One, great in pow'r, Strong in thy might, All the world
Glad-ly we call! Deep to deep now replies, At thy command, All the world
Glad-ly above! Greater than all thy work—Thy living Word! All the world
Glad-ly be giv'n! Father, Son, Ho-ly Ghost, One God on high! Evermore

CHORUS.

made by thee, Darkness and light. Praise, . . . O praise the Migh-ty One,
made by thee, Ocean and land.
saved by thee, Through Christ the Lord.
evermore, Earth sea and sky. Praise, O Praise, Praise the Mighty One,

Wor — — — — — — — — — ship and a-dore, ...
Worship and a-dore, Worship and a-dore,

Sing — — — — — ing of his glo — — — — ry, Now and ev-ermore.
Singing of his glo — ry, Singing of his glory,

Copyright, 1891, by Wm. J. Kirkpatrick.

14. What Time I Am Afraid.

"What time I am afraid, I will trust in thee."—Ps. xxxvi: 3.

Miss J. H. Johnston.   "Scotch." Arr. by P. Bilhorn.

1. Sometimes the sky is o-vercast, I fear to lose my way;
2. Ac-cu-sing conscience, like a flame, With-in my spir-it burns,
3. From all the unknown fu-ture days My tim-id heart re-coils,
3. When twilight shadows soft-ly fall, And night comes on a-pace,

Un-til the storm be o-ver-past, Oh, keep my heart, I pray.
The tempt-er speaks of wrath and shame, My heart in anguish turns
But known to God are all his ways, And all my cares and toils;
In life and death, O Lord of all, I would be-hold thy face.

In darkness, dan-ger, and in doubt, My heart is sore dismayed,
To him whose blood a-tones for me, On whom my heart is stayed,
The wisdom, pow'r, and might are thine, But mine the promised aid,
The fi-nal hour, oh, let me meet In peace, and un-dis-mayed,

But "I will trust in thee, O Lord, What time I am a-fraid."
For "I will trust in thee, O Lord, What time I am a-fraid."
And "I will trust in thee, O Lord, What time I am a-fraid."
For "I will trust in thee, O Lord, What time I am a-fraid."

Copyright, 1888, by P. Bilhorn.

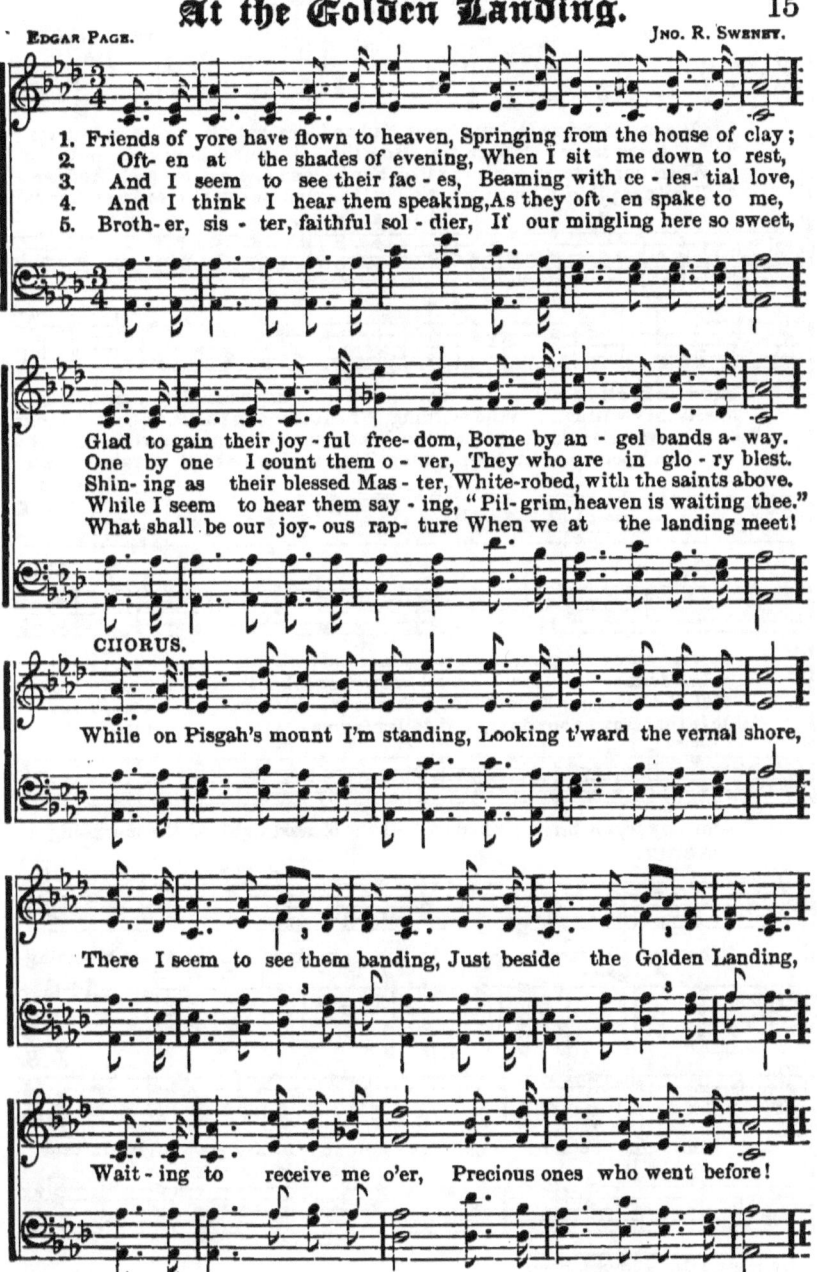

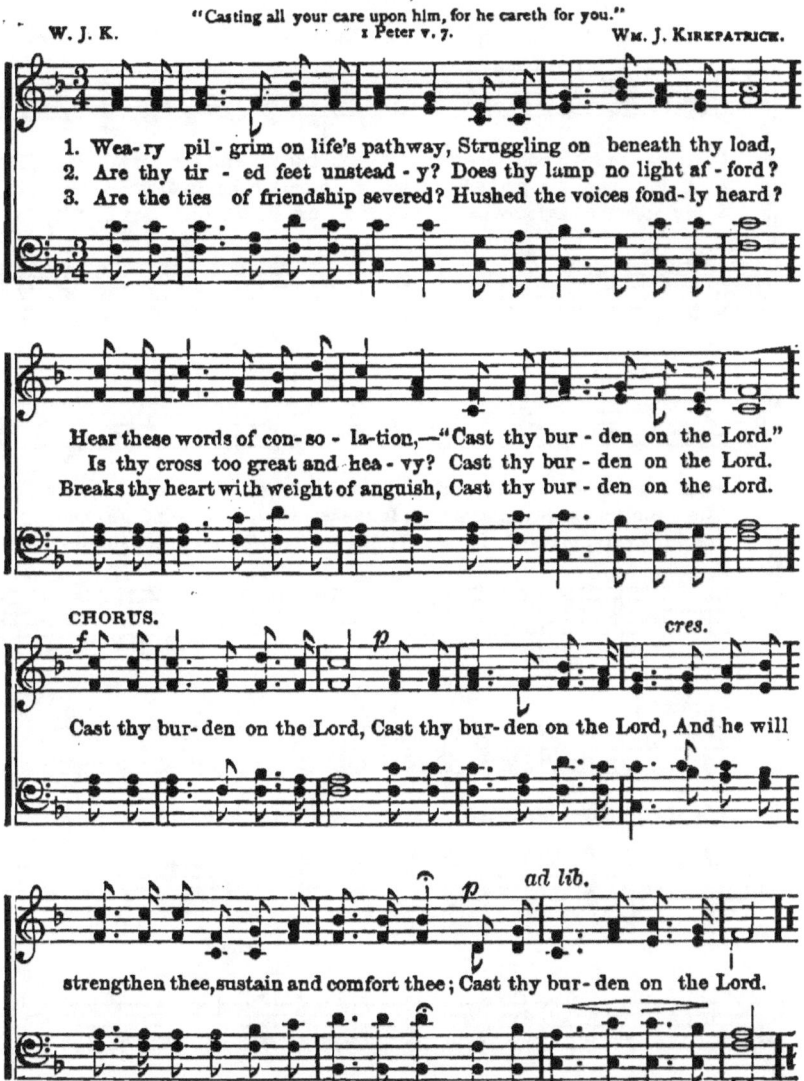

Cast thy Burden on the Lord.

"Casting all your care upon him, for he careth for you."
1 Peter v. 7.

W. J. K.
Wm. J. Kirkpatrick.

1. Wea-ry pil-grim on life's pathway, Struggling on beneath thy load,
2. Are thy tir-ed feet unstead-y? Does thy lamp no light af-ford?
3. Are the ties of friendship severed? Hushed the voices fond-ly heard?

Hear these words of con-so-la-tion,—"Cast thy bur-den on the Lord."
Is thy cross too great and hea-vy? Cast thy bur-den on the Lord.
Breaks thy heart with weight of anguish, Cast thy bur-den on the Lord.

CHORUS.

Cast thy bur-den on the Lord, Cast thy bur-den on the Lord, And he will strengthen thee, sustain and comfort thee; Cast thy bur-den on the Lord.

4 Does thy heart with faintness falter?
Does thy mind forget his word?
Does thy strength succumb to weak-
Cast thy burden on the Lord. [ness?

5 He will hold thee up from falling,
He will guide thy steps aright;
He will strengthen each endeavor;
He will keep thee by his might.

Copyright, 1880, by Jno. J. Hood. *Temple Songs*—B

Never Alone.

ROSSITER W. RAYMOND. FERD. SILCHER.

1. Far out on the des-o-late bil-low The sail-or sails the sea,
2. Far down in the earth's dark bo-som The min-er mines the ore;
3. Forth in-to the dread-ful bat-tle The steadfast sol-dier goes,
4. Lord, grant, as we sail life's o-cean, Or delve in its mines of woe,

A-lone with the night and the tempest, Where countless dan-gers be;
Death lurks in the dark be-hind him, And hides in the rock be-fore;
No friend, when he lies a-dy-ing, His eyes to kiss and close;
Or fight in the ter-ri-ble con-flict, This com-fort all to know:

REFRAIN.

Yet nev-er a-lone is the Christian Who lives by faith and prayer;
4th v.—That never a-lone, etc.

For God is a Friend un-fail-ing, And God is ev-'ry-where.

Sound the Battle Cry.

W. F. S.   WM. F. SHERWIN. By per.

Vigorously, in march time.

1. Sound the bat-tle cry, See! the foe is nigh; Raise the standard high For the Lord; Gird your ar-mor on, Stand firm ev-'ry one, Rest your cause up-on his ho-ly word. Rouse, then, sol-diers!
2. Strong to meet the foe, March-ing on we go, While our cause we know Must pre-vail; Shield and ban-ner bright, Gleam-ing in the light, Bat-tling for the right, we ne'er can fail.
3. Oh! thou God of all, Hear us when we call, Help us, one and all, By thy grace; When the bat-tle's done, And the vic-t'ry won, May we wear the crown be-fore thy face.

CHORUS.

2d CHO.—*Rouse, then, freemen,*

ral-ly round the banner! Ready, stead-y, pass the word a-long; Onward, forward, shout a-loud, Ho-san-na! Christ is Captain of the migh-ty throng.

come from hill and valley; Fathers, brothers, earnest, brave, and strong! Onward forward, all u-nit-ed ral-ly, "Death to Alchohol!" your bat-tle song.

The New Song.—CONCLUDED.

reign; ... Glo-ry and praise to the Lamb that was slain.
that shall reign;

3 Can my lips be mute, or my heart be sad,
When the gracious Master hath made me glad?
When he points where the many mansions be,
And sweetly says, 'There is one for thee'?

4 I shall catch the gleam of its jasper wall
When I come to the gloom of the evenfall,
For I know that the shadows, dreary and dim,
Have a path of light that will lead to him.

From "Gems of Praise," by per.

Fill Me Now.

Rev. E. H. Stokes, D.D.　　　　　　　　　Jno. R. Sweney.

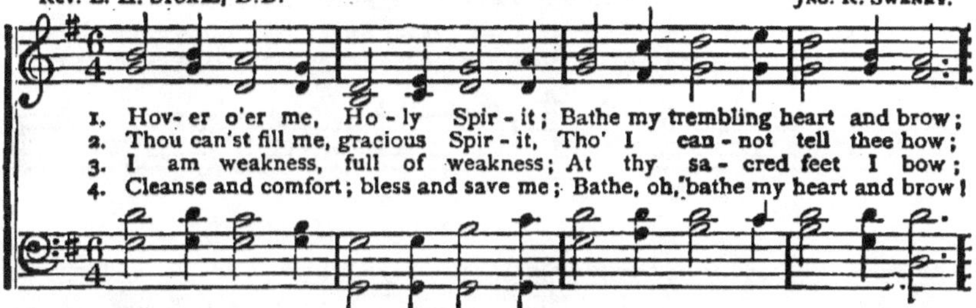

1. Hov-er o'er me, Ho-ly Spir-it; Bathe my trembling heart and brow;
2. Thou can'st fill me, gracious Spir-it, Tho' I can-not tell thee how;
3. I am weakness, full of weakness; At thy sa-cred feet I bow;
4. Cleanse and comfort; bless and save me; Bathe, oh, bathe my heart and brow!

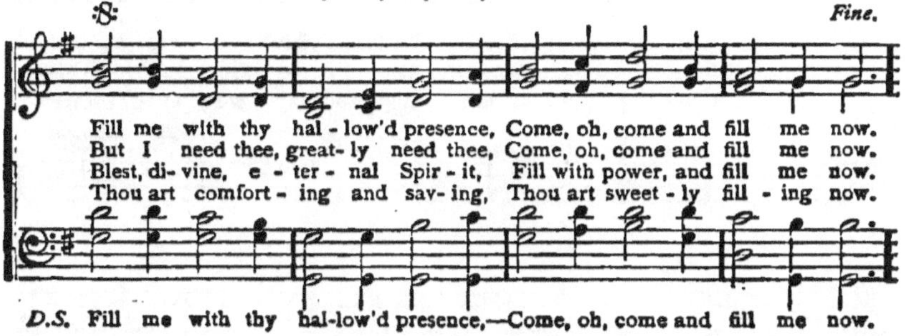

Fill me with thy hal-low'd presence, Come, oh, come and fill me now.
But I need thee, great-ly need thee, Come, oh, come and fill me now.
Blest, di-vine, e-ter-nal Spir-it, Fill with power, and fill me now.
Thou art comfort-ing and sav-ing, Thou art sweet-ly fill-ing now.

D.S. Fill me with thy hal-low'd presence,—Come, oh, come and fill me now.

CHORUS.　　　　　　　　　　　　　　　　　　　　D.S.

Fill me now, fill me now, Je-sus, come, and fill me now;

Copyright, 1879, by John J. Hood.

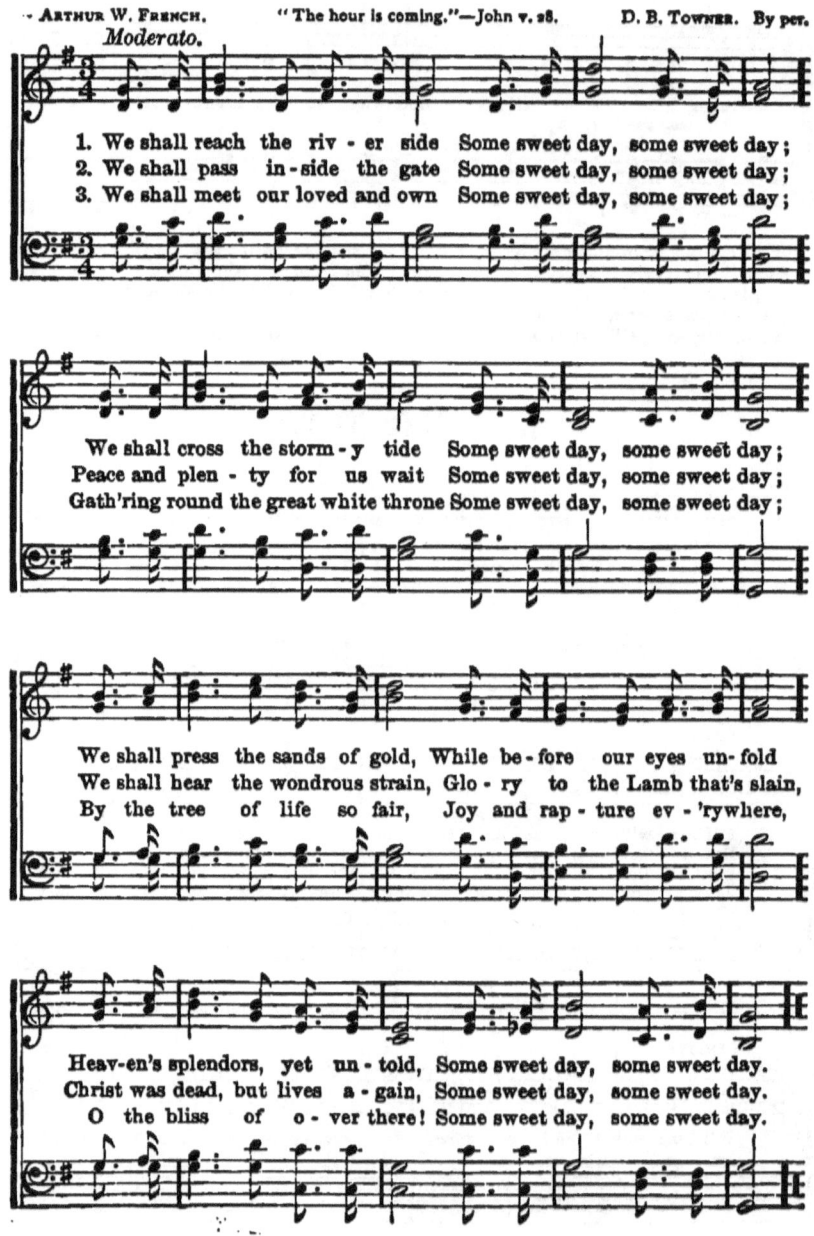

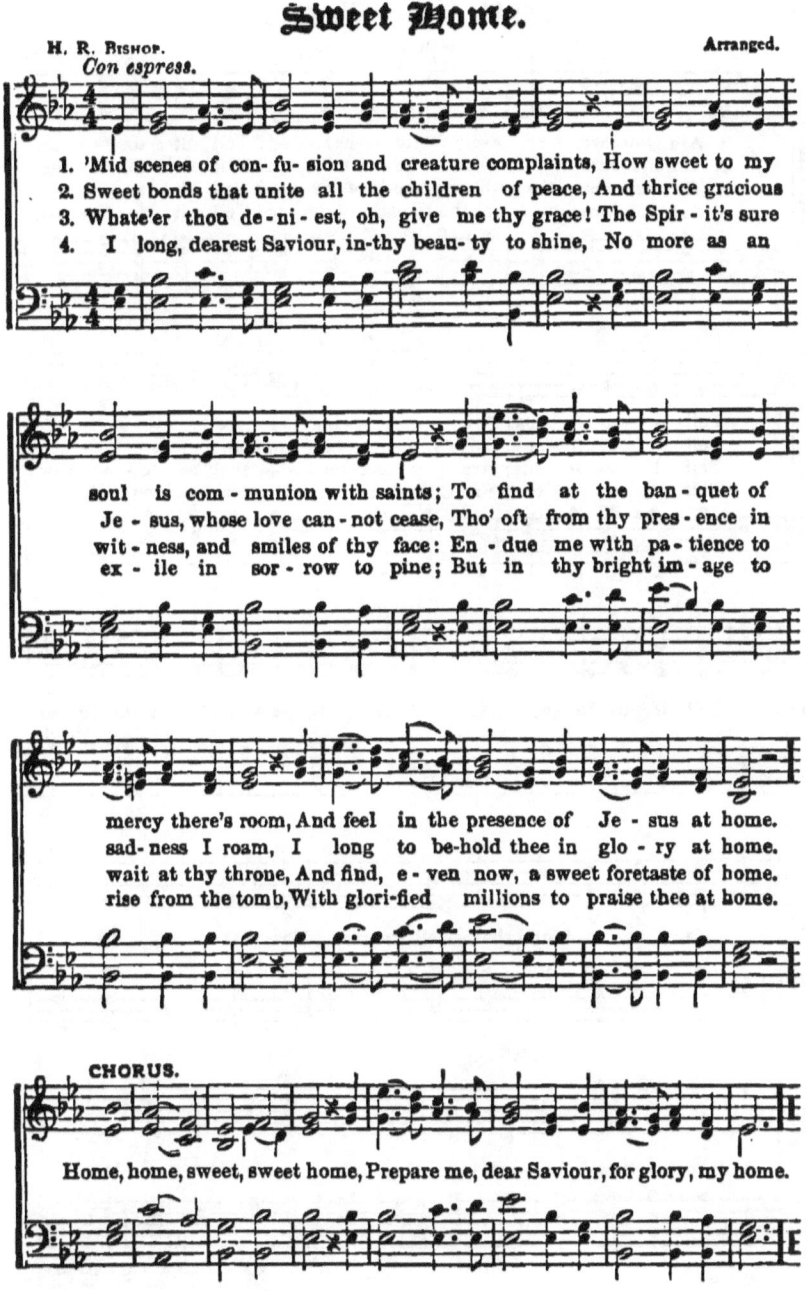

28. Tell it to Jesus.

J. E. Rankin, D. D. — Matt. xiv. 12. — E. S. Lorenz.

1. Are you wea-ry, are you heavy-heart-ed? Tell it to Je-sus,
2. Do the tears flow down your cheeks unbidden? Tell it to Je-sus,
3. Do you fear the gath'ring clouds of sor-row? Tell it to Je-sus,
4. Are you trou-bled at the thought of dy-ing? Tell it to Je-sus,

Tell it to Je-sus; Are you griev-ing o-ver joys de-part-ed?
Tell it to Je-sus; Have you sins that to man's eye are hid-den?
Tell it to Je-sus; Are you anx-ious what shall be to-mor-row?
Tell it to Je-sus; For Christ's coming Kingdom are you sigh-ing?

CHORUS.

Tell it to Je-sus a-lone. Tell it to Je-sus, Tell it to Je-sus, He is a friend that's well known; You have no oth-er such a friend or broth-er, Tell it to Je-sus a-lone.

By permission.

Is not this the Land of Beulah. 31

ANON. ARRANGED.

1. I am dwelling on the mountain, Where the gold-en sunlight gleams
2. I can see far down the mountain, Where I wandered wea-ry years,
3. I am drinking at the fountain, Where I ev-er would a-bide;

O'er a land whose wondrous beauty Far ex-ceeds my fondest dreams,
Oft-en hindered in my journey By the ghosts of doubts and fears,
For I've tast-ed life's pure riv-er, And my soul is sat-is-fied;

Where the air is pure e-the-real, La-den with the breath of flowers,
Brok-en vows and dis-appointments Thickly sprinkled all the way,
There's no thirsting for life's pleasures, Nor a-dorn-ing, rich and gay,

CHO.—Is not this the land of Beulah, Blessed, bless-ed land of light,

D.S. Chorus.

They are blooming by the fountain,'Neath the am-a-ranthine bowers.
But the Spir-it led, un-er-ring, To the land I hold to-day.
For I've found a rich-er treasure, One that fad-eth not a-way.

Where the flow-ers bloom for-ev-er, And the sun is always bright.

4 Tell me not of heavy crosses,
  Nor the burdens hard to bear,
For I've found this great salvation
  Makes each burden light appear;
And I love to follow Jesus,
  Gladly counting all but dross,
Worldly honors all forsaking
  For the glory of the Cross.

5 Oh, the Cross has wondrous glory!
  Oft I've proved this to be true;
When I'm in the way so narrow
  I can see a pathway through;
And how sweetly Jesus whispers:
  Take the Cross, thou need'st not fear,
For I've tried this way before thee,
  And the glory lingers near.

Blessed be the Fountain.—CONCLUDED.

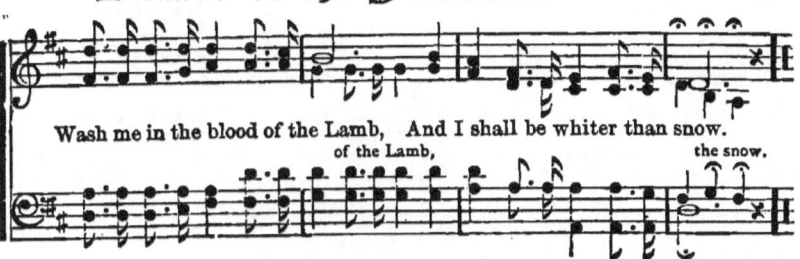

Give me Jesus.

Arr. by W. J. K.

1. When I'm hap-py, hear me sing, When I'm happy, hear me sing, When I'm
2. When in sor-row, hear me pray, When in sorrow, hear me pray, When in
3. When I'm dy-ing, hear me cry, When I'm dying, hear me cry, When I'm
4. When I'm ris-ing, hear me shout, When I'm rising, hear me shout, When I'm
5. When in heav-en, we will sing, When in heav-en, we will sing, When in

CHORUS.

hap-py, hear me sing, Give me Je - sus, Give me Je - sus, Give me Je - sus; You may have all the world: Give me Je - sus.
sorrow, hear me pray, Give me Je - sus,
dying, hear me cry, Give me Je - sus,
rising, hear me shout, Give me Je - sus,
heaven, we will sing, Blessed Je - sus, Bles-sed Je - sus, Bles-sed Je - sus, By thy grace we are saved, Bles-sed Je - sus.

Copyright, 1885, by John J. Hood.

 —CONCLUDED.

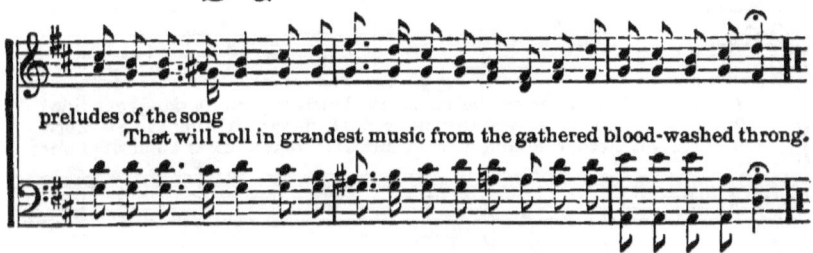

preludes of the song
That will roll in grandest music from the gathered blood-washed throng.

More Faith in Jesus.

HENRIETTA E. BLAIR. WM. J. KIRKPATRICK.

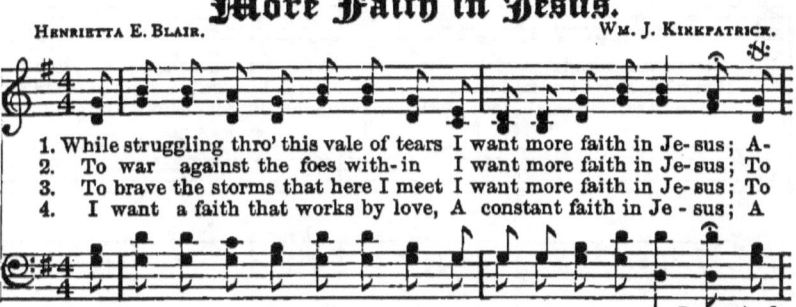

1. While struggling thro' this vale of tears I want more faith in Je-sus; A-
2. To war against the foes with-in I want more faith in Je-sus; To
3. To brave the storms that here I meet I want more faith in Je-sus; To
4. I want a faith that works by love, A constant faith in Je-sus; A

D. S.—And

Fine. CHORUS.

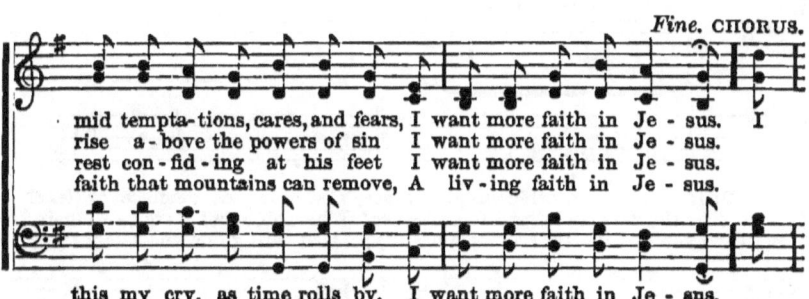

mid tempta-tions, cares, and fears, I want more faith in Je - sus. I
rise a-bove the powers of sin I want more faith in Je - sus.
rest con-fid-ing at his feet I want more faith in Je - sus.
faith that mountains can remove, A liv-ing faith in Je - sus.

this my cry, as time rolls by, I want more faith in Je - sus.

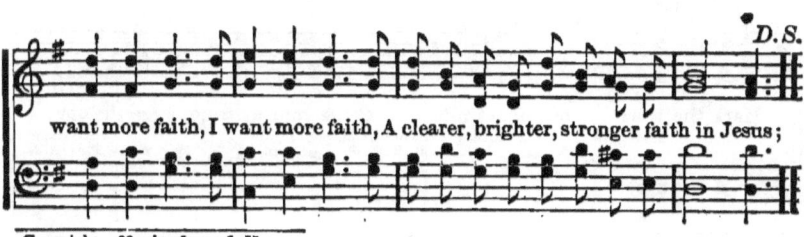

want more faith, I want more faith, A clearer, brighter, stronger faith in Jesus;

Copyright, 1885, by JOHN J. HOOD.

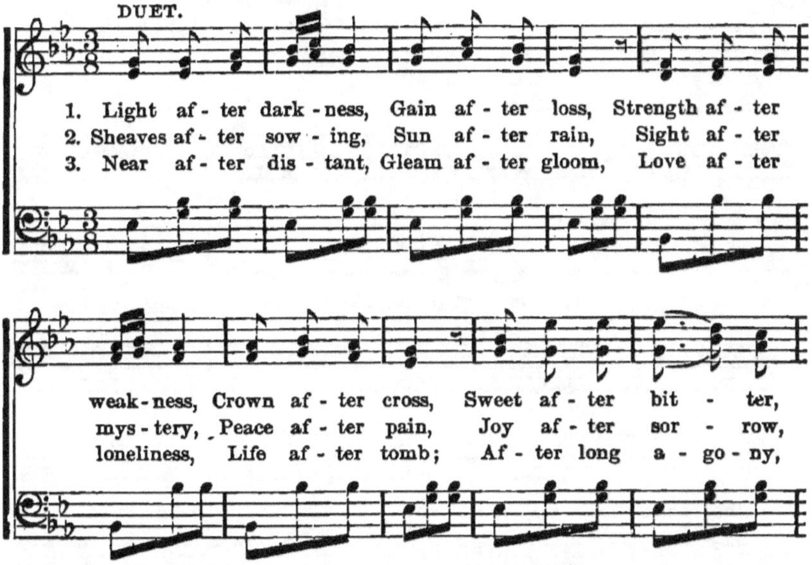

46. Glory to Jesus, He Saves.

P. B.
P. BILHORN.

1. Glo-ry to Je-sus who died on the tree, Paid the great price that my soul might be free; Now I can sing hal-le-lu-jah to God,
2. Once in my heart there was sin and despair, Now the dear Saviour him-self dwelleth there, And from his pres-ence comes peace to my soul,
3. Come, then, ye wea-ry, who long to be free, Come to the Saviour, he wait-eth for thee; Then with the ransomed this song you can sing,

CHORUS.

Glo-ry! he saves, he saves. Glo-ry! he saves, glo-ry! he saves, Saves a poor sin-ner like me; Glo-ry! he saves, glo-ry! he saves, Saves a poor sin-ner like me. like me.

Copyright, 1885, by P. Bilhorn.

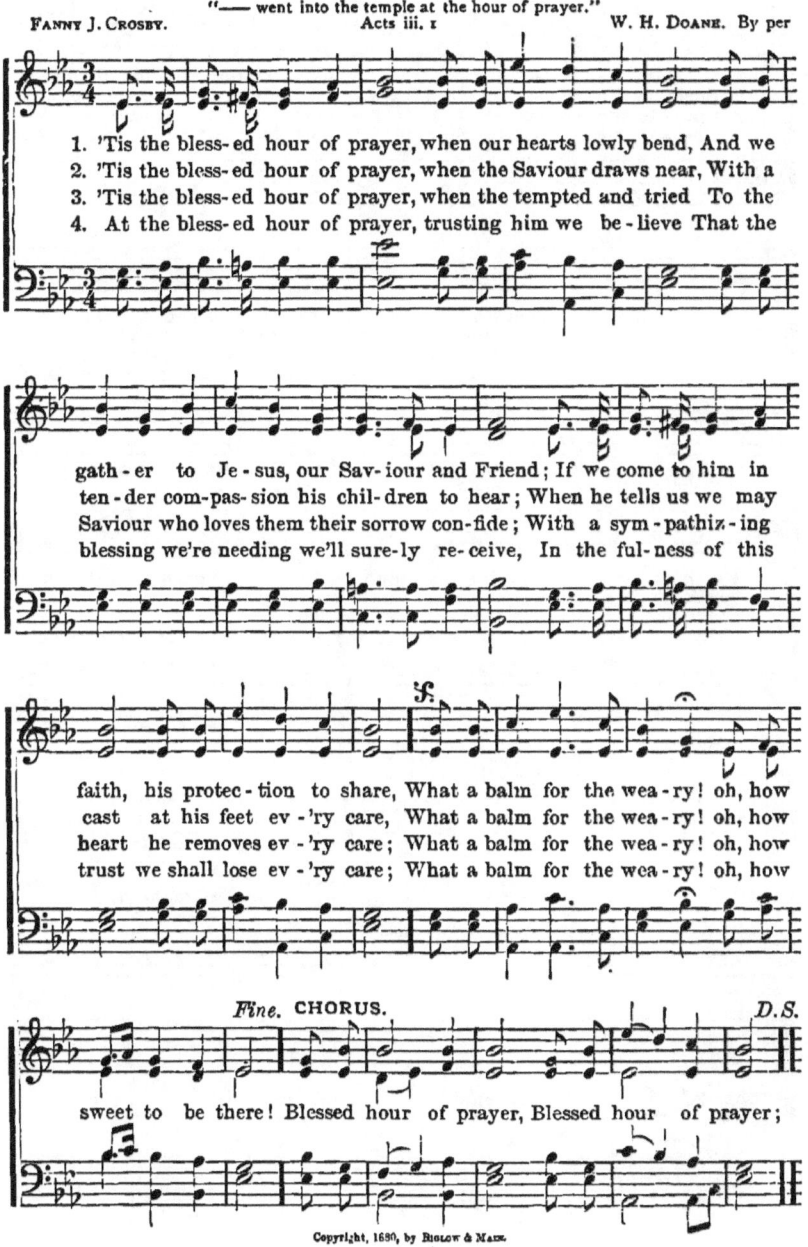

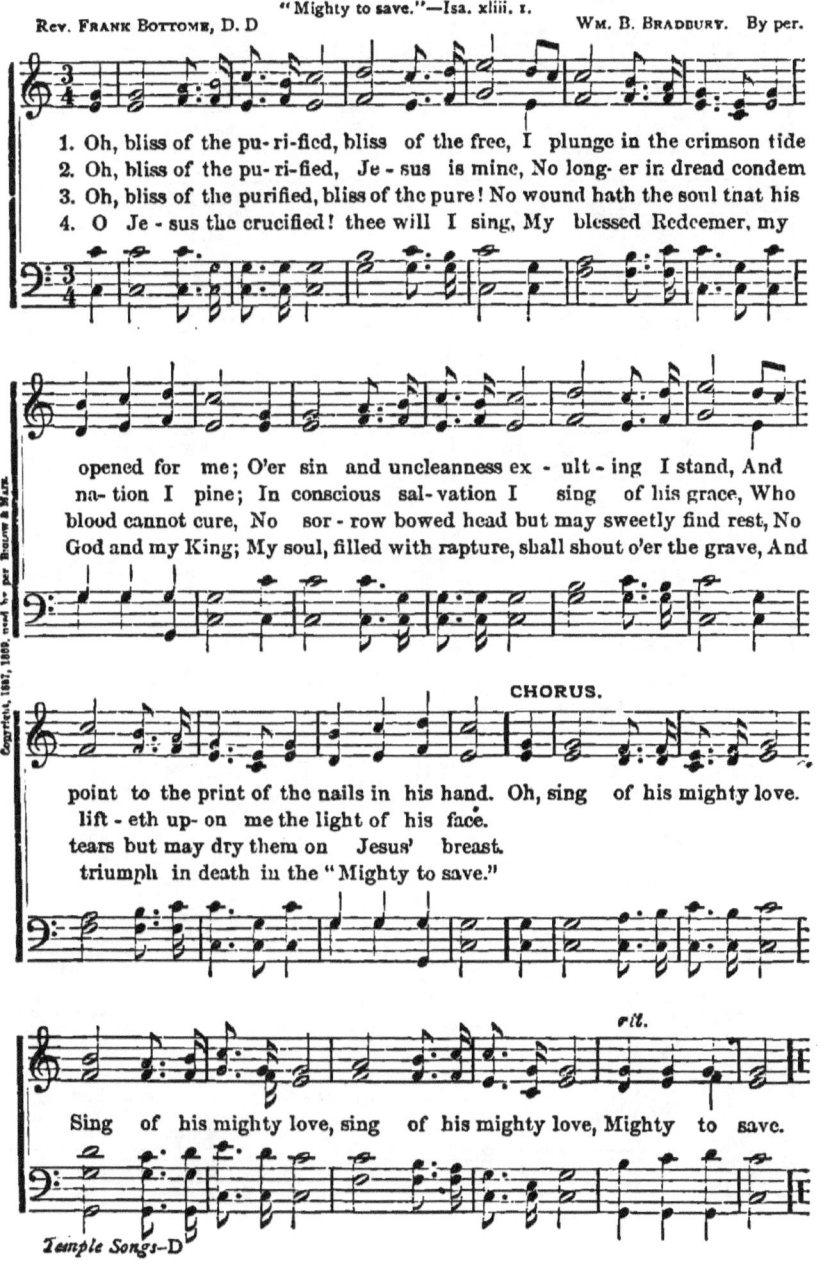

The Future.—CONCLUDED.

I'll Live for Him.

C. R. Dunbar.

By permission.

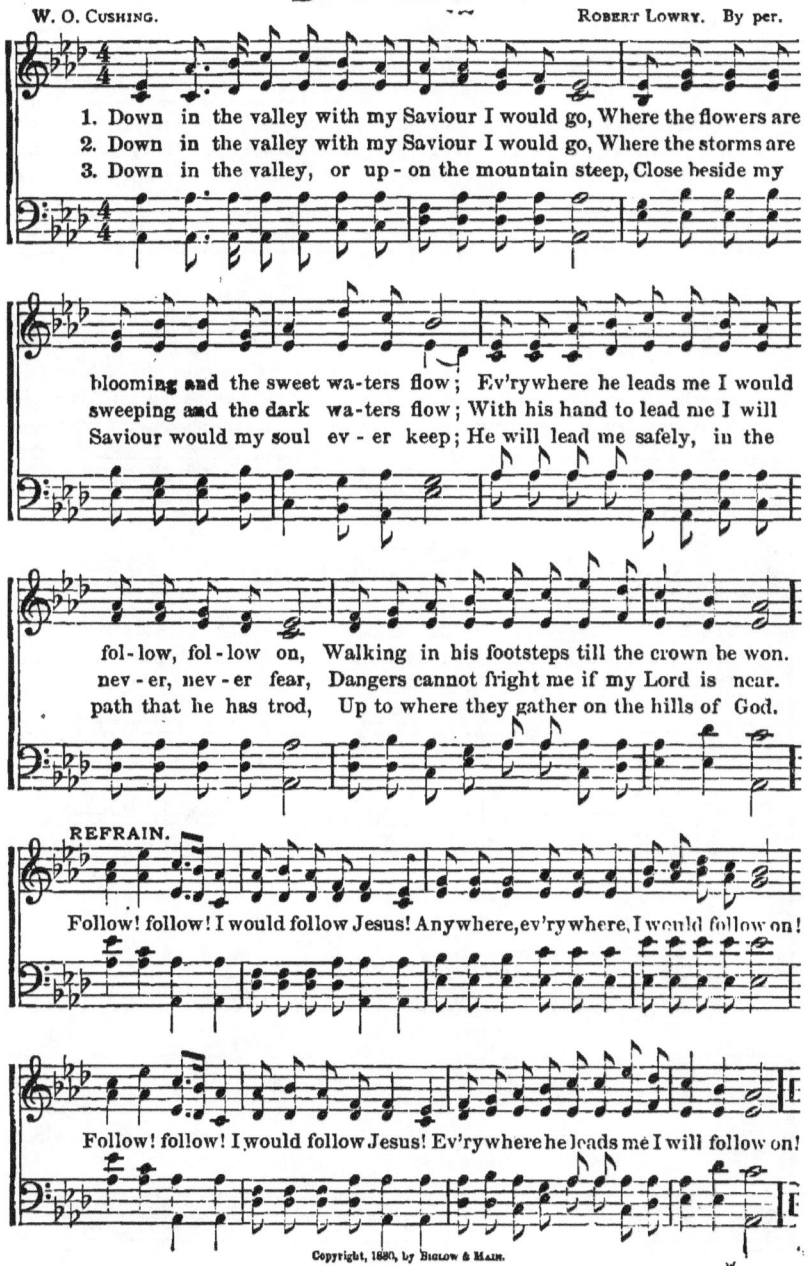

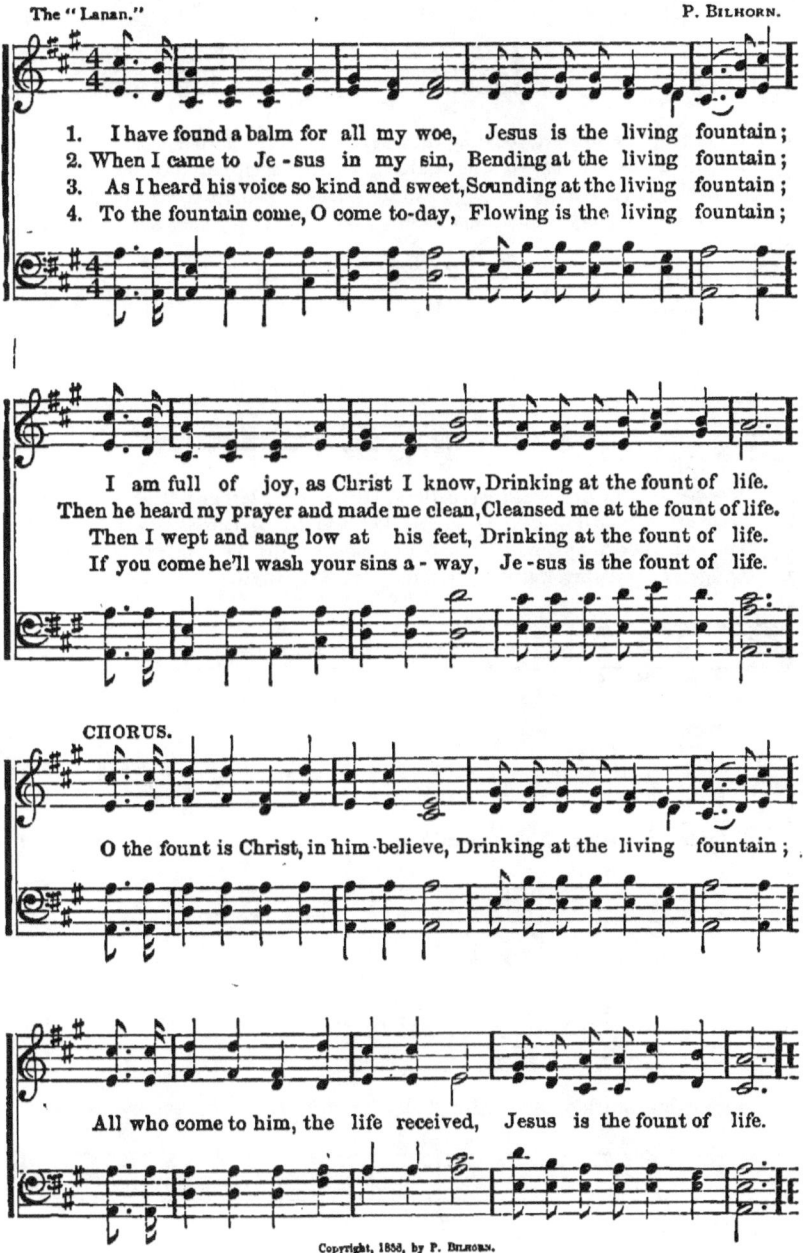

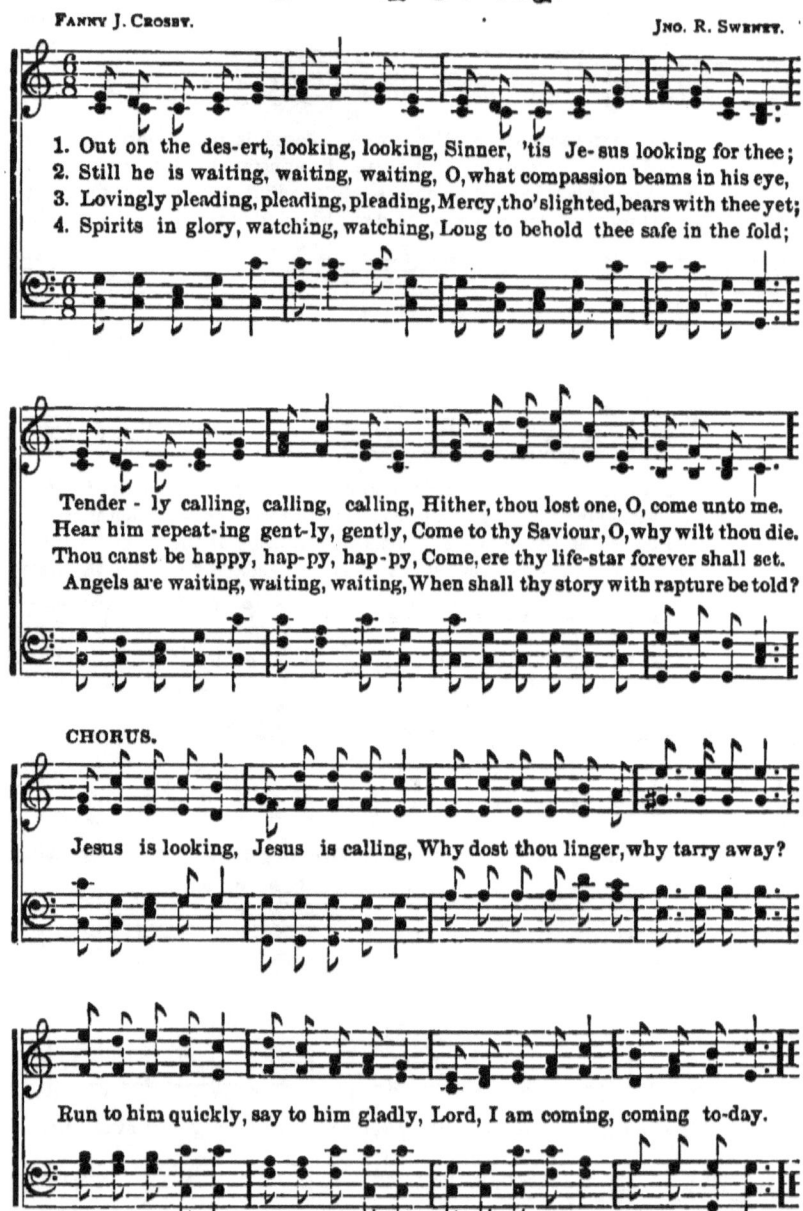

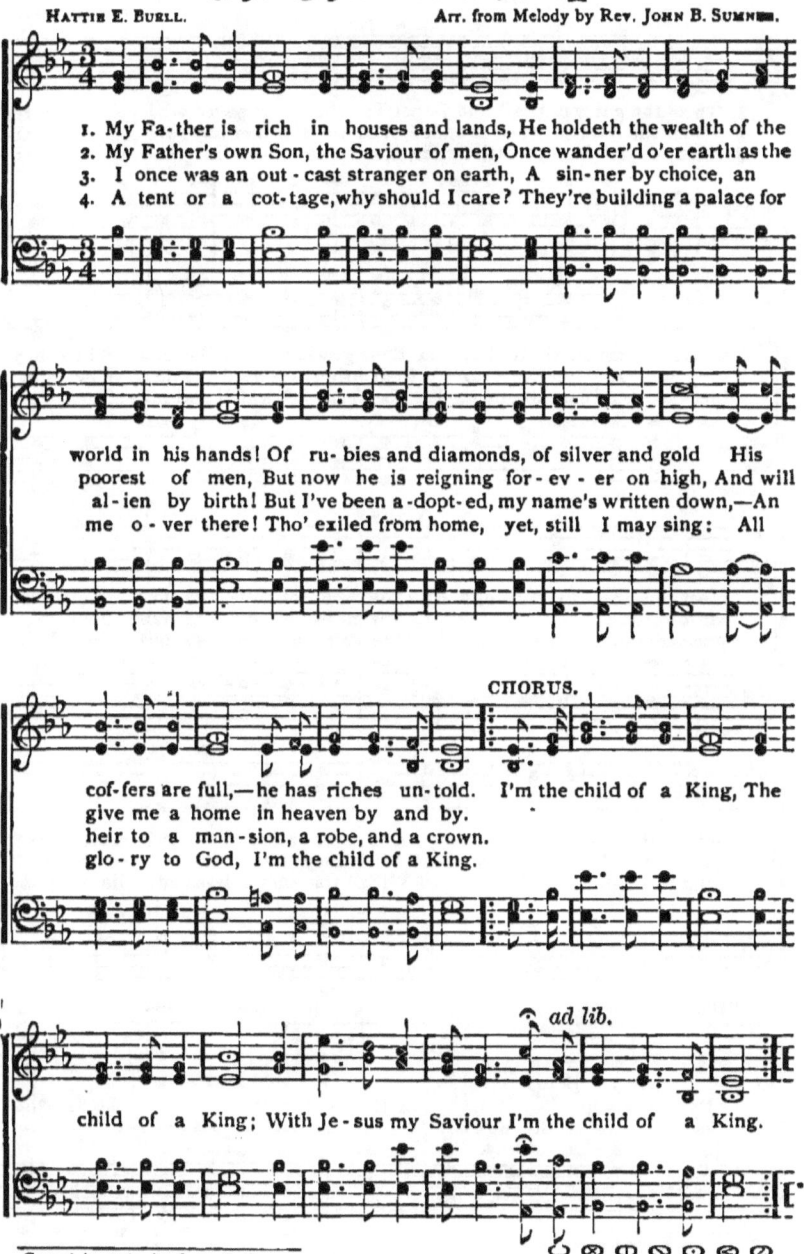

2 I wandered on in the darkness,
  Not a ray of light could I see,
  And the thought filled my heart with sadness,
  There's no hope for a sinner like me.

3 I then fully trusted in Jesus,
  And oh, what a joy came to me;
  My heart was filled with his praises,
  For saving a sinner like me.

4 No longer in darkness I'm walking,
  For the light is now shining on me,
  And now unto others I'm telling,
  How he saved a poor sinner like me.

5 And when life's journey is over,
  And I the dear Saviour shall see,
  I'll praise him forever and ever,
  For saving a sinner like me.

Copyright, 1881, by JOHN J. HOOD.

Happy Tidings.

LIZZIE EDWARDS. JNO. R. SWENEY.

1. Tidings, happy tidings, Hark! hark! the sound! Hear the joyful ech-o
2. Tidings, happy tidings, Hark! hark! they say, Do not slight the warning,
3. Tidings, happy tidings, Hark! hark! a-gain! Rushing o'er the mountain,

Thro' the world resound; Christ the Lord proclaims them, Hear and heed the call,
Come, oh, come to-day; Christ, our loving Saviour, Still repeats the call,
Sweeping o'er the plain; Onward goes the message, 'Tis the Saviour's call,

REFRAIN.

Come, ye starving ones that perish, Room, room for all. Whosoev-er asketh,
Come, ye weary, heavy-laden, Room, room for all.
Come, for ev'rything is ready, Room, room for all.

Jesus will receive; Whosoever thirsteth, Jesus will relieve; See the living

waters, Flowing full and free; Oh, the blessed whosoev-er! That means me.

Copyright, 1882, by Jno. R. Sweney.

5. Ho! all ye heavy-laden, come!
   Here's pardon, comfort, rest, and home.
   Ye wanderers from a Father's face,
   Return, accept his proffered grace.
   Ye tempted ones, there's refuge nigh:
   "Jesus of Nazareth passeth by."

6. But if you still this call refuse,
   And all his wondrous love abuse,
   Soon will he sadly from you turn,
   Your bitter prayer for pardon spurn.
   "Too late! too late!" will be the cry—
   "Jesus of Nazareth *has passed by.*"

62. Anchored On the Rock of Ages.

F. L. Cornish. "This is my Rest forever."—Psalm cxxxii: 14. Jno. R. Sweney.

1. Resting in the love of Jesus, Sweetly rest - - ing ev'ry day, Anchored on the Rock of A - ges, Till the shad - - ows flee a - way.
2. I can hear the surges tread - ing Up and down life's storm - y beach, But up - on this sure Founda - tion I am far beyond their reach.
3. Here is ev - - er-lasting com - fort, Here is found the sweet - est peace, Here I shall a - bide in pa - tience, Till life's storms for - ev - er cease.

CHORUS.

I am resting, sweetly resting, Resting, happy, happy all the day, Anchored on... the Rock of A - ges, Till the shad - - ows flee a - way.

(Anchored on the / Till the shad - ows)

Copyright, 1891, by Jno. R. Sweney.

The Lily of the Valley.

English Melody, arranged

1. I have found a friend in Jesus, he's ev'rything to me, He's the fairest of ten thousand to my soul; The Li-ly of the Valley, in him alone I see All I need to cleanse and make me fully whole; In sorrow he's my comfort, in trouble he's my stay, He tells me ev'ry care on him to roll. He's the

2. He all my griefs has taken, and all my sorrows borne; In temptation he's my strong and mighty tower; I have all for him forsaken, and all my idols torn From my heart, and now he keeps me by his power; Tho' all the world forsake me, and Satan tempts me sore, Thro' Jesus I shall safely reach the goal. He's the

3. He will never, never leave me, nor yet forsake me here, While I live by faith and do his blessed will; A wall of fire about me, I've nothing now to fear; With his manna he my hungry soul shall fill; Then sweeping up to glo-ry to see his blessed face, Where rivers of delight shall ever roll. He's the

D. S.—Lily of the Valley, the bright and Morning Star, He's the fair-est of ten thousand to my soul. Cho.—In sorrow, etc. *(after each verse.)*

Copyright, 1885, by John J. Hood.

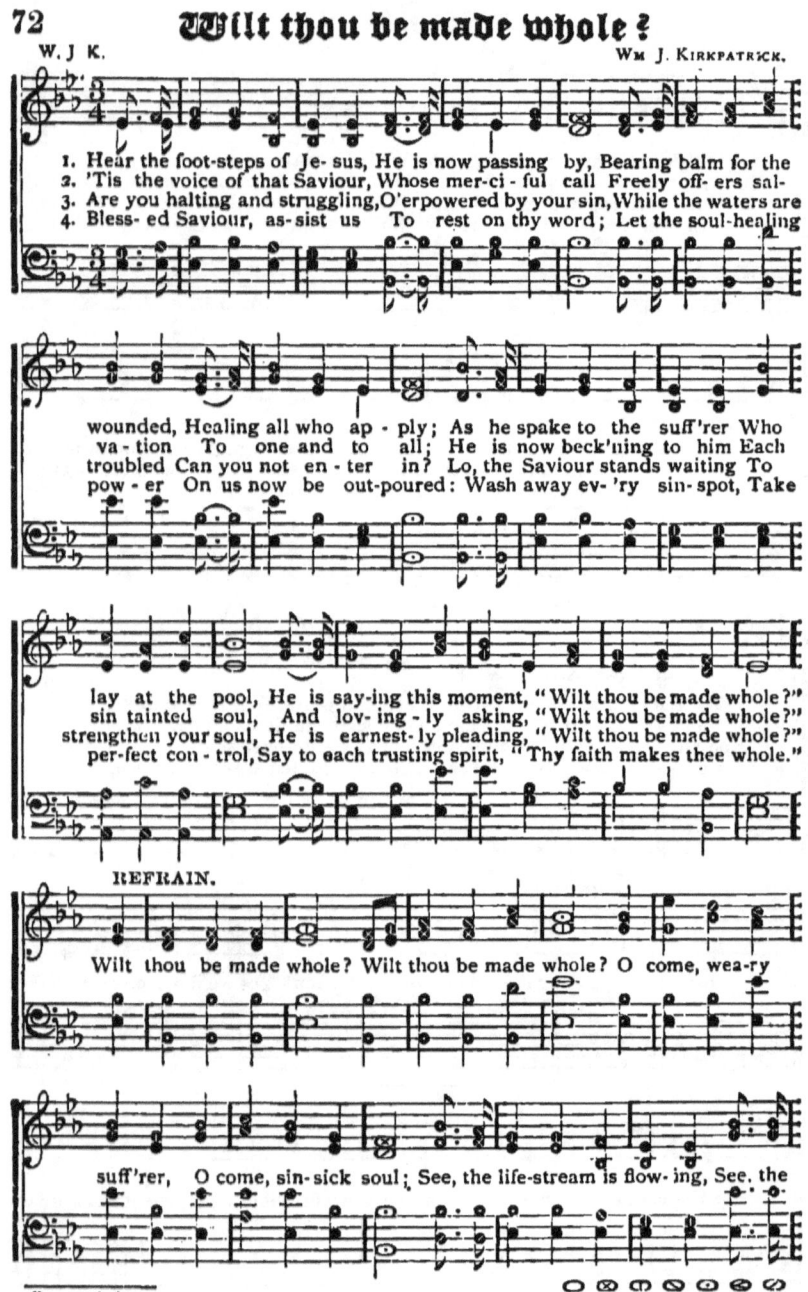

Wilt thou be made whole?—CONCLUDED. 73

cleansing waves roll, Step in-to the cur-rent and thou shalt be whole.

Glorious Fountain.

COWPER.   T. C. O'KANE.

1. There is a fountain filled with blood, filled with blood, filled with blood, There is a fount-ain filled with bood, Drawn from Imman-uel's veins,
And sinners plung'd beneath that flood, beneath that flood, beneath that flood, And sinners plunged beneath that flood, Lose all their guilt-y stains.

2. The dy-ing thief rejoiced to see, rejoiced to see, rejoiced to see, The dy-ing thief rejoiced to see That fount-ain in his day,
And there may I, tho' vile as he, tho' vile as he, tho' vile as he, And there may I, tho' vile as he, Wash all my sins a-way.

CHORUS.

Oh, glo-ri-ous fount-ain! Here will I stay, And in thee ev-er Wash my sins a-way.

3 Thou dying Lamb, ‖: thy precious blood :‖
Shall never lose its power,
Till all the ransomed ‖:Church of God:‖
Are saved, to sin no more.

4 E'er since by faith ‖: I saw the stream ‖
Thy flowing wounds supply,
Redeeming love ‖: has been my theme,:‖
And shall be till I die.

From "Redeemer's Praise," by per.

DO RE MI FA SO LA SI

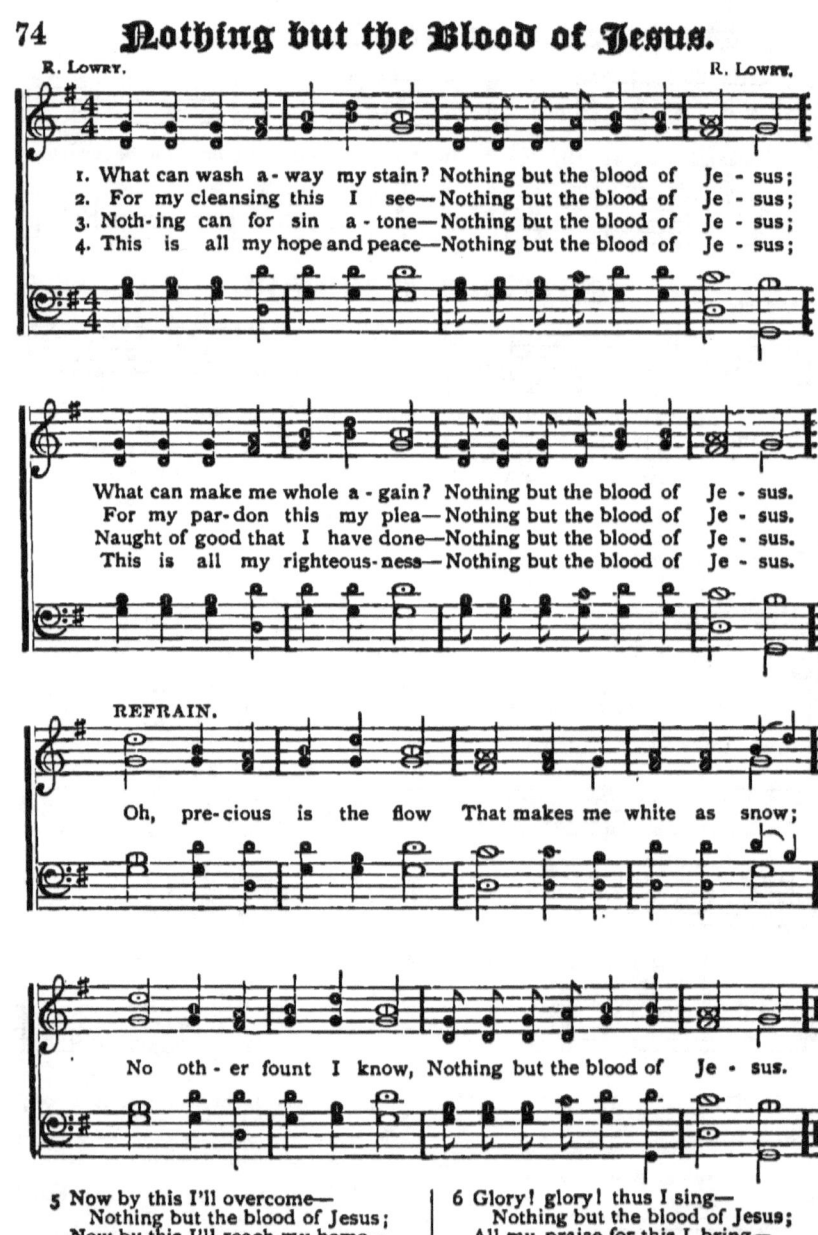

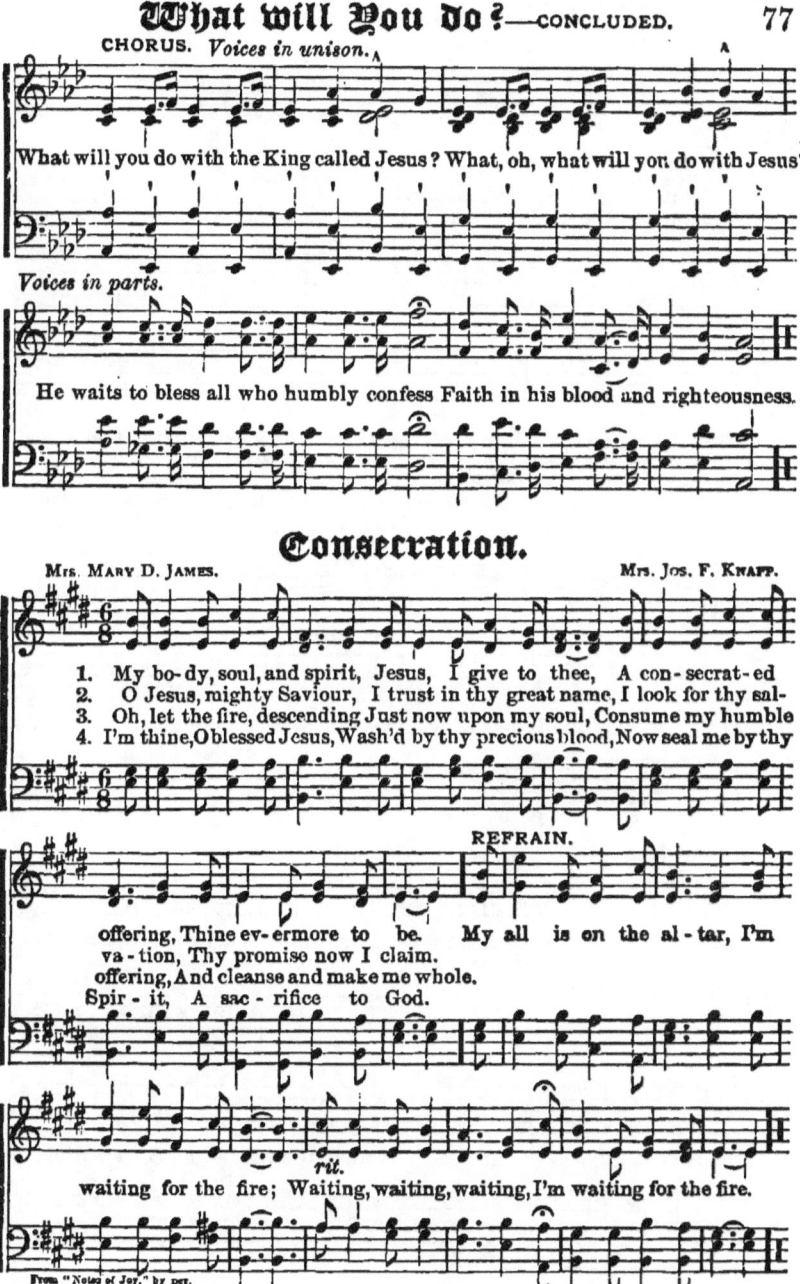

Take me as I am.

Charlotte Elliott. **JUST AS I AM.** *Tune and Chorus above.*

1 Just as I am, without one plea,
 But that thy blood was shed for me,
 And that thou bid'st me come to thee,
  O Lamb of God, I come!

2 Just as I am, and waiting not
 To rid my soul of one dark blot,
 To thee whose blood can cleanse each
  O Lamb of God, I come! [spot,

3 Just as I am, though tossed about
 With many a conflict, many a doubt,
 Fightings within, and fears without,
  O Lamb of God, I come!

4 Just as I am—poor, wretched, blind;
 Sight, riches, healing of the mind,
 Yea, all I need, in thee to find,
  O Lamb of God, I come!

5 Just as I am—thou wilt receive,
 Wilt welcome, pardon, cleanse, relieve;
 Because thy promise I believe,
  O Lamb of God, I come!

6 Just as I am—thy love unknown
 Hath broken every barrier down,
 Now, to be thine, yea, thine alone,
  O Lamb of God, I come!

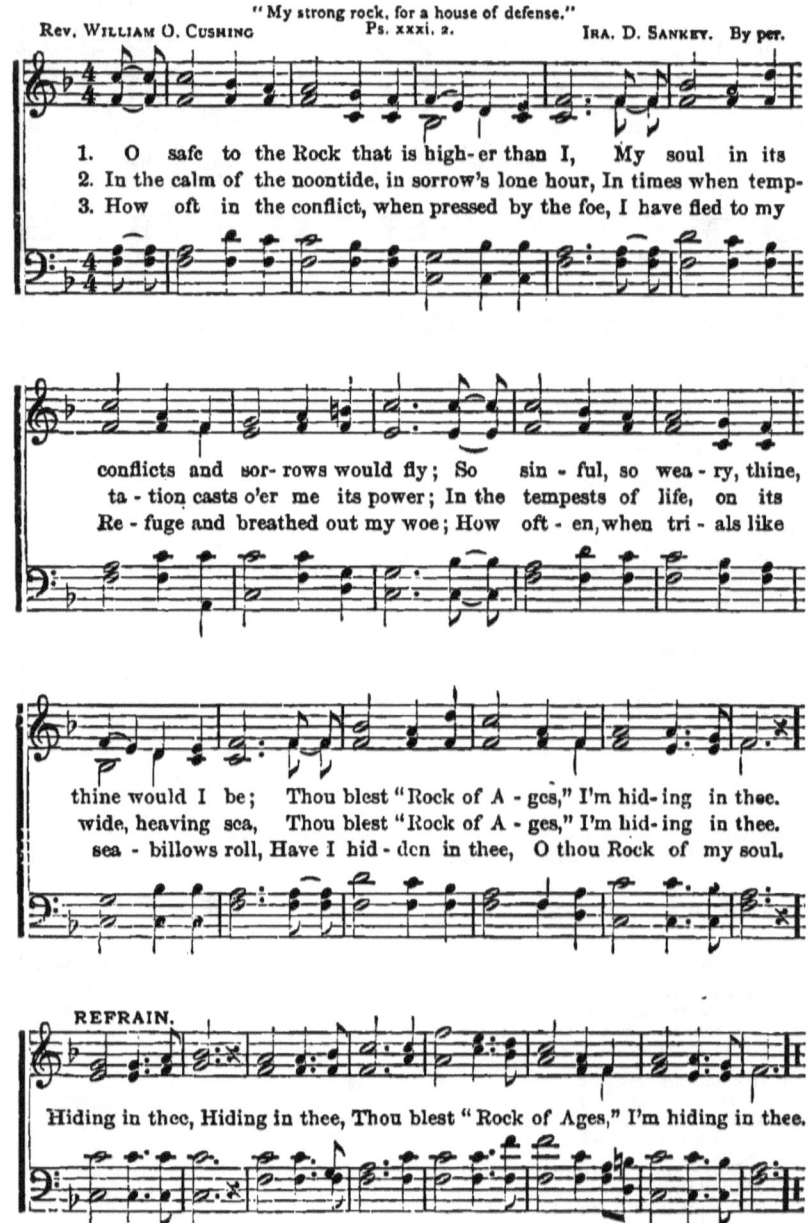

The Great Physician.

2. Your many sins are all forgiven,
   Oh, hear the voice of Jesus;
   Go on your way in peace to heaven,
   And wear a crown with Jesus.

3. All glory to the dying Lamb!
   I now believe in Jesus;
   I love the blessed Saviour's name,
   I love the name of Jesus.

4. The children too, both great and small,
   Who love the name of Jesus,
   May now accept his gracious call
   To work and live for Jesus.

5. Come, brethren, help me sing his praise,
   Oh, praise the name of Jesus;
   Come, sisters, all your voices raise,
   Oh, bless the name of Jesus.

6. His name dispels my guilt and fear,
   No other name but Jesus;
   Oh, how my soul delights to hear
   The precious name of Jesus.

7. And when to that bright world above,
   We rise to see our Jesus,
   We'll sing around the throne of love
   His name, the name of Jesus.

MY SOUL, BE ON THY GUARD.—Laban, key D.

1. My soul, be on thy guard,
   Ten thousand foes arise;
   The hosts of sin are pressing hard
   To draw thee from the skies.

2. Oh, watch, and fight, and pray;
   The battle ne'er give o'er;
   Renew it boldly every day,
   And help divine implore.

3. Ne'er think the vict'ry won,
   Nor lay thine armor down;
   The work of faith will not be done
   Till thou obtain the crown.

4. Then persevere till death
   Shall bring thee to thy God;
   He'll take thee, at thy parting breath,
   To his divine abode.

Though Your Sins be as Scarlet.

"Though your sins be as scarlet, they shall be as white as snow."—Isaiah i. 18.

FANNY J. CROSBY. W. H. DOANE. By per.

DUET. *Gently.*

1. "Tho' your sins be as scarlet, They shall be as white as snow; as snow:
2. Hear the voice that entreats you, Oh, return ye unto God! to God!
3. He'll forgive your transgressions, And remember them no more; no more;

QUARTET.

Tho' they be red . . . . like crimson, They shall be as wool;"
He is of great . . . compassion, And of wondrous love;
"Look un- to me, . . . ye people," Saith the Lord your God;

Tho' they be red

DUET. *p*   QUARTET. *f*

"Tho' your sins be as scarlet, Tho' your sins be as scarlet,
Hear the voice that entreats you, Hear the voice that entreats you,
He'll forgive your transgressions, He'll forgive your transgressions,

p ritard.

They shall be as white as snow, They shall be as white as snow."
Oh, return ye un-to God! Oh, return ye un-to God!
And remem- ber them no more, And remem- ber them no more.

Copyright, 1887, by W. H. Doane.

Seeking to Save.

87

"For the Son of Man is come to seek and to save that which was lost."
Luke xix. 10.

P. P. B.   P. P. Bliss.

1. Ten-der-ly the Shepherd, O'er the mountains cold, Goes to bring his
2. Patient-ly the own-er Seeks with earnest care, In the dust and
3. Lov-ing-ly the Fa-ther Sends the news a-round: "He once dead now

CHORUS.

lost one Back to the fold. Seek-ing to save, Seek-ing to save,
darkness Her treasure rare.
liv-eth—Once lost is found."

Lost one, 'tis Je-sus Seek-ing to save: Seek-ing to save,

Seek-ing to save, Lost one, 'tis Je-sus Seek-ing to save.

By permission of The John Church Co., owners of copyright.

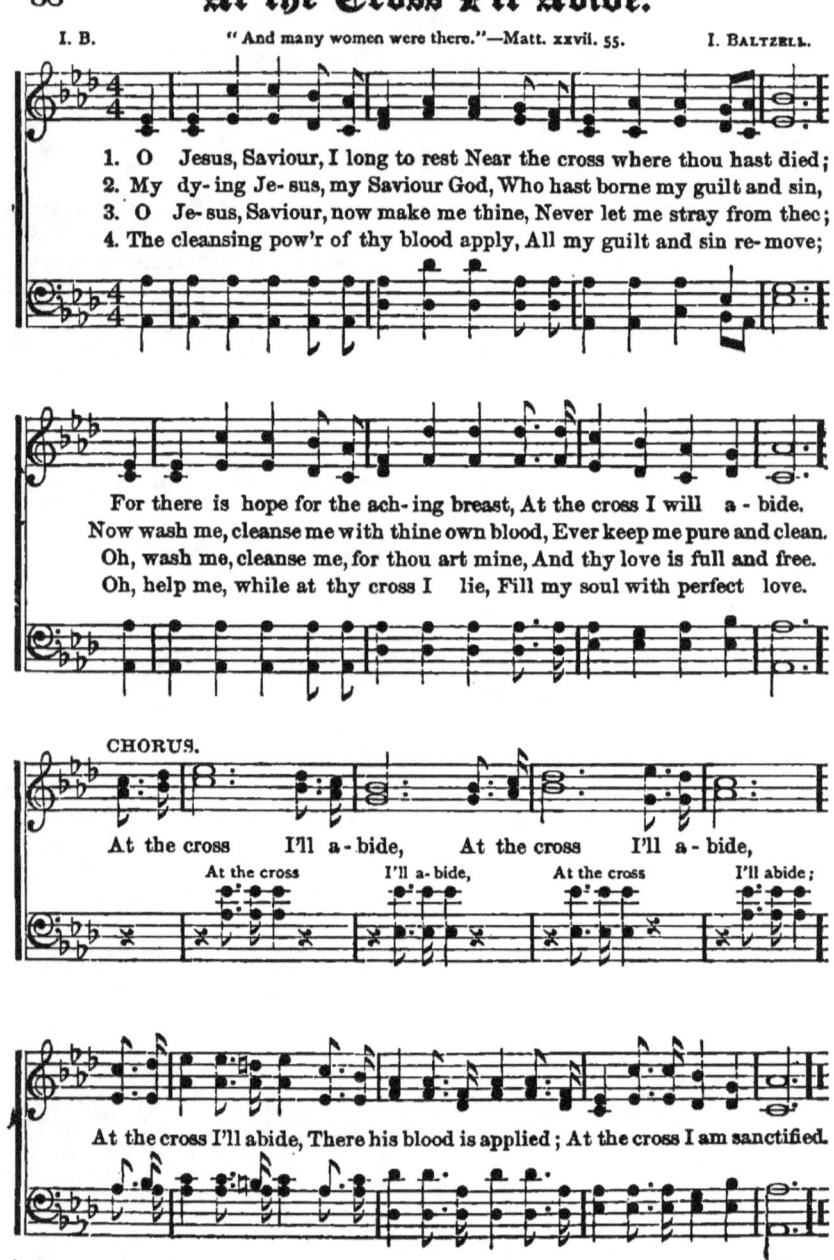

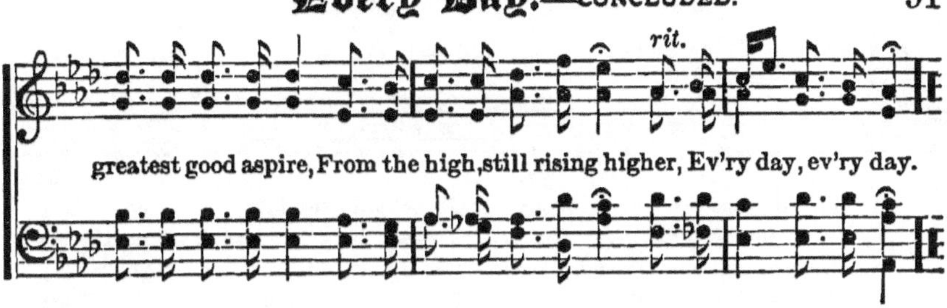

Every Day.—CONCLUDED. 91

greatest good aspire, From the high, still rising higher, Ev'ry day, ev'ry day.

Jesus, I come to Thee.

FANNY J. CROSBY.   WM. J. KIRKPATRICK.

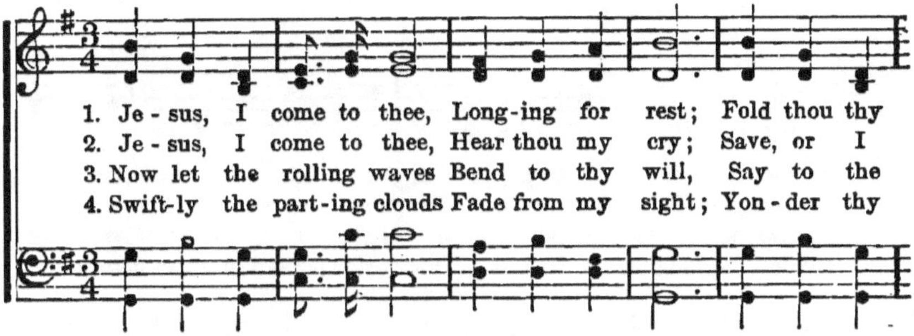

1. Je-sus, I come to thee, Long-ing for rest; Fold thou thy
2. Je-sus, I come to thee, Hear thou my cry; Save, or I
3. Now let the rolling waves Bend to thy will, Say to the
4. Swift-ly the part-ing clouds Fade from my sight; Yon-der thy

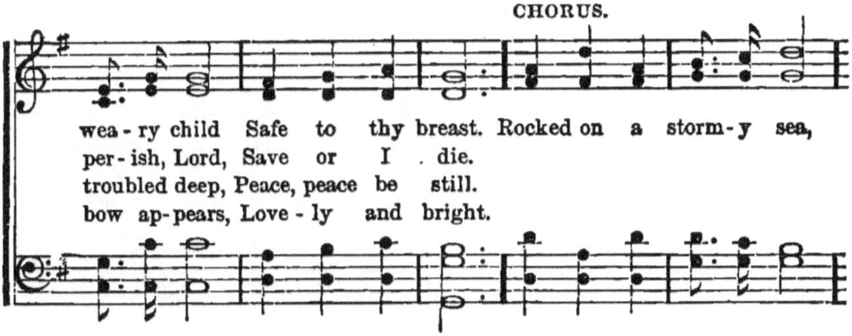

CHORUS.

wea-ry child Safe to thy breast. Rocked on a storm-y sea,
per-ish, Lord, Save or I die.
troubled deep, Peace, peace be still.
bow ap-pears, Love-ly and bright.

Oh, be not far from me, Lord, let me cling to thee, On-ly to thee.

Copyright, 1884, by JOHN J. HOOD.

94. Is there Any One Here.

MARTHA J. LANKTON. WM. J. KIRKPATRICK.

1. Is there an-y one here that is will-ing to-day On Je-sus the Lord to be-lieve? Is there an-y poor soul that is longing to-day The gift of his grace to re-ceive.
2. Is there an-y one here that is try-ing to-day The fet-ters of e-vil to break? An-y read-y to fol-low the Saviour to-day, And take up the cross for his sake.
3. Is there an-y one here that is wea-ry to-day, Or la-den, or sor-row oppressed? Is there any sad heart that is praying to-day To find in the Sav-iour a rest.
4. Hear the Saviour's sweet voice while he calls thee again, O come, and be-lieve and o-bey; He is waiting to bless, he will comfort thee now! He nev-er turned an-y a-way.

CHORUS.

Come un-to me, Come un-to me; Je-sus is call-ing, call-ing now to thee, Come, oh, come un-to me.

Copyright, 1886, by JOHN J. HOOD.

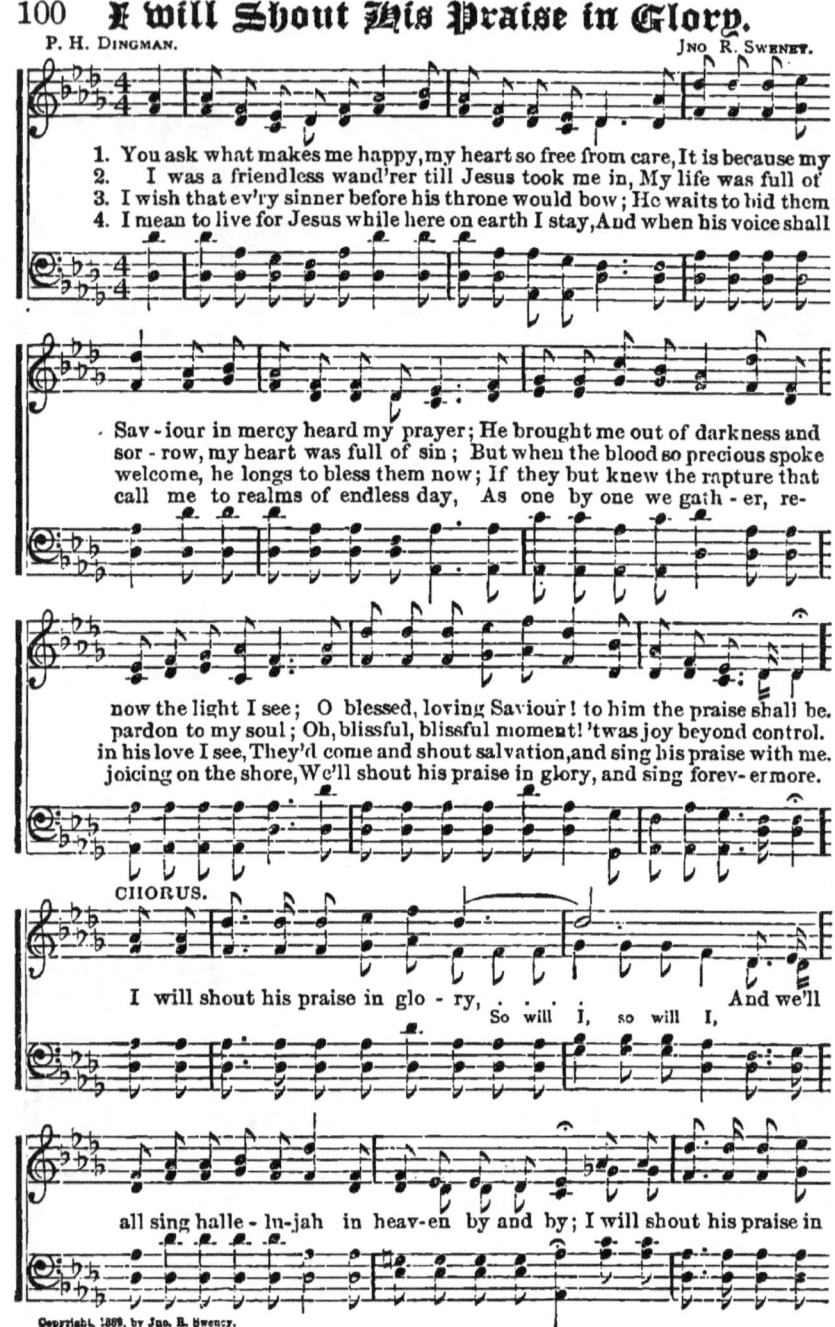

The Land Just Across the River.

T. C. O'KANE. By per.

1. On Jordan's stormy banks I stand, And cast a wishful eye
2. O'er all these wide-extended plains Shines one eternal day;
3. When shall I reach that happy place, And be forever blest?
4. Filled with delight, my raptured soul Would here no longer stay;

To Canaan's fair and happy land, Where my possessions lie.
There God the Son forever reigns, And scatters night away.
When shall I see my Father's face, And in his bosom rest?
Tho' Jordan's waves around me roll, Fearless I'd launch away.

CHORUS.

We will rest in the fair and happy land, by and by, Just across on the evergreen shore, .. evergreen shore.

Sing the song of Moses and the Lamb, by and by, And dwell with Jesus evermore.

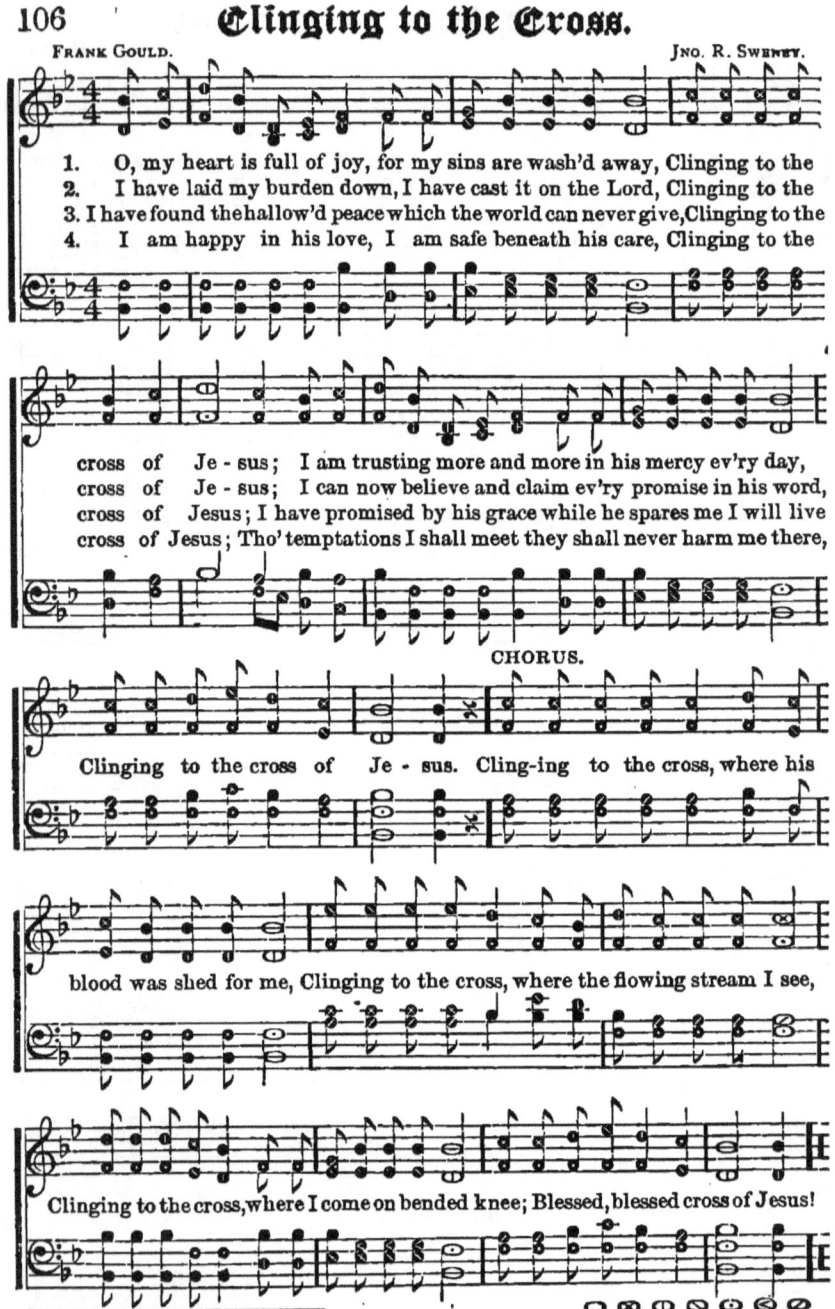

108. The Mind of Jesus.

E. E. Hewitt.
Jno. R. Sweney.

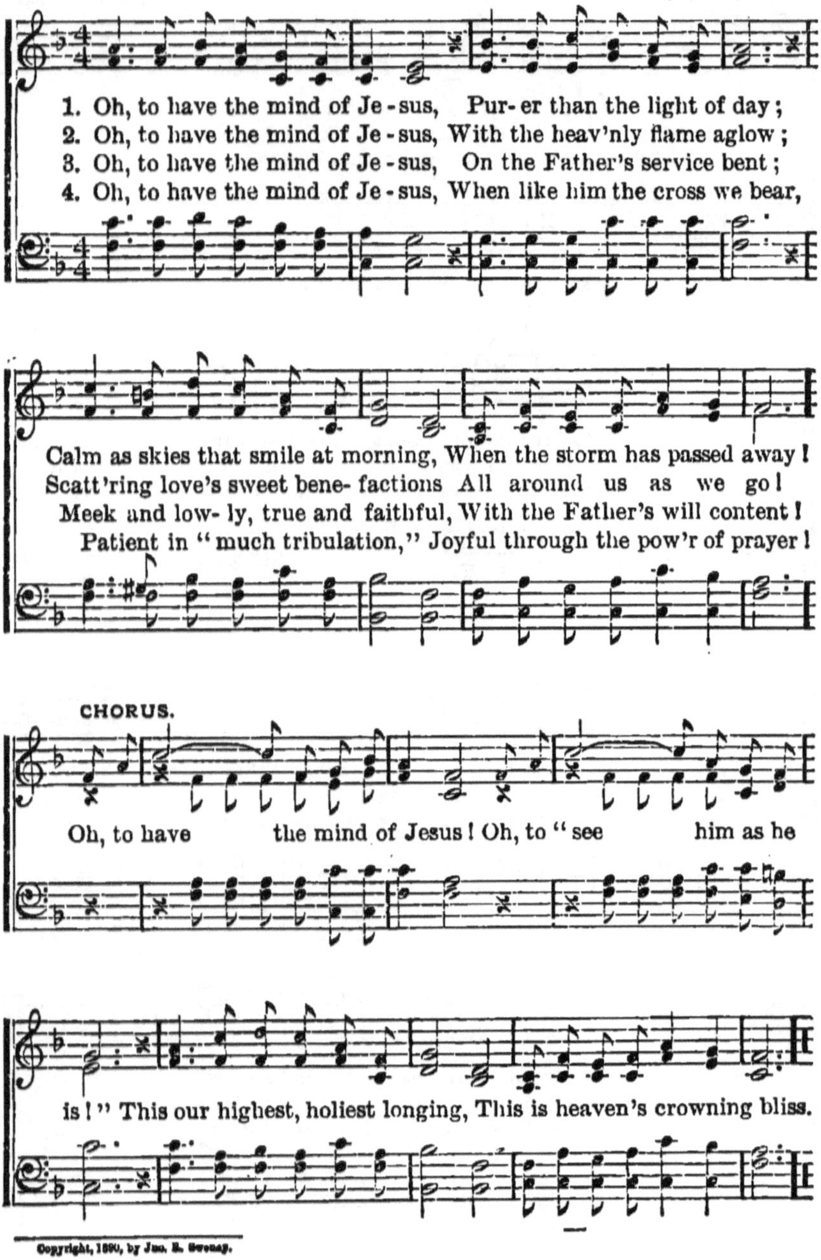

1. Oh, to have the mind of Je-sus, Pur-er than the light of day;
2. Oh, to have the mind of Je-sus, With the heav'nly flame aglow;
3. Oh, to have the mind of Je-sus, On the Father's service bent;
4. Oh, to have the mind of Je-sus, When like him the cross we bear,

Calm as skies that smile at morning, When the storm has passed away!
Scatt'ring love's sweet bene-factions All around us as we go!
Meek and low-ly, true and faithful, With the Father's will content!
Patient in "much tribulation," Joyful through the pow'r of prayer!

CHORUS.

Oh, to have the mind of Jesus! Oh, to "see him as he is!" This our highest, holiest longing, This is heaven's crowning bliss.

Copyright, 1890, by Jno. R. Sweney.

He Came to Save Me.

HENRIETTA E. BLAIR. WM. J. KIRKPATRICK.

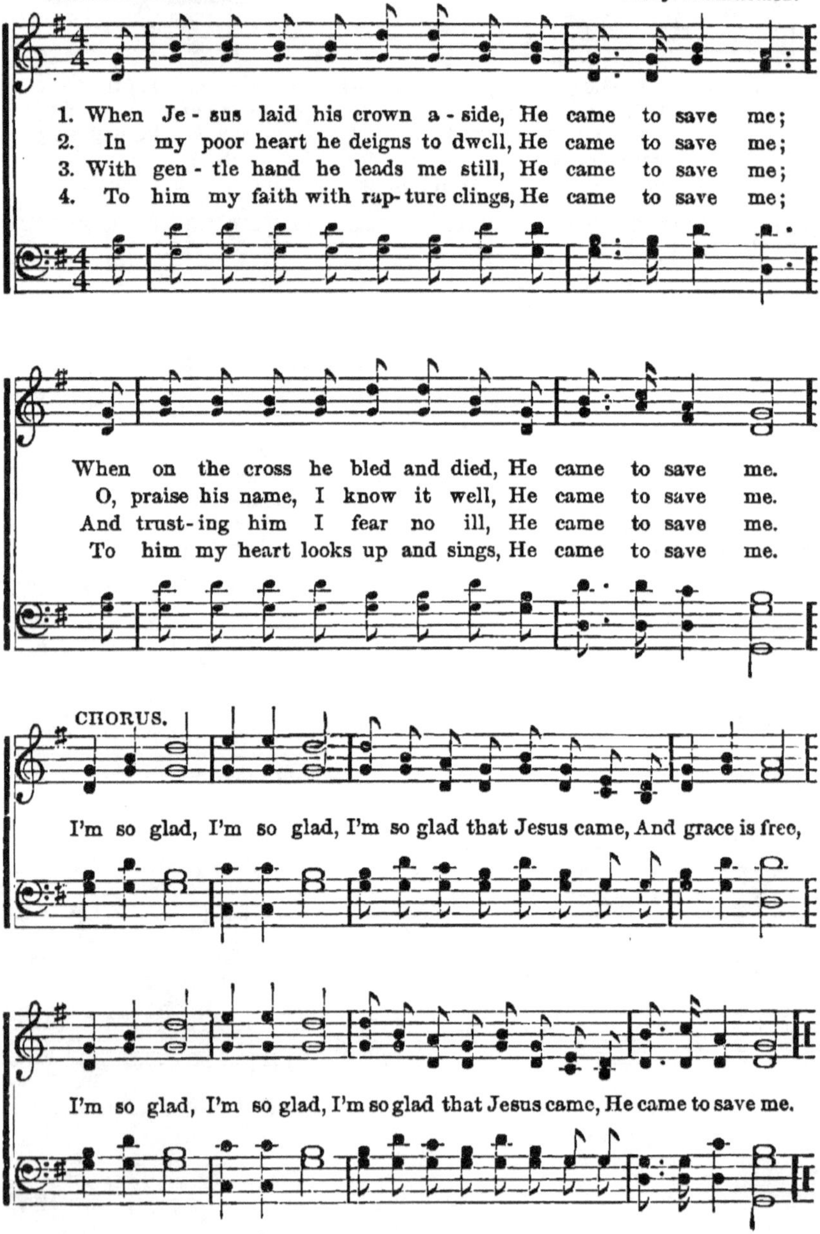

Will You Go?—CONCLUDED.

saints are clothed in white? Go where the saved shall find no night, But endless day?

I will Trust in Thee.

In answer to question of leader at Ocean Grove "Who will trust?" many rose, saying, "I will."

W. H. G.
W. H. GEISTWEIT.

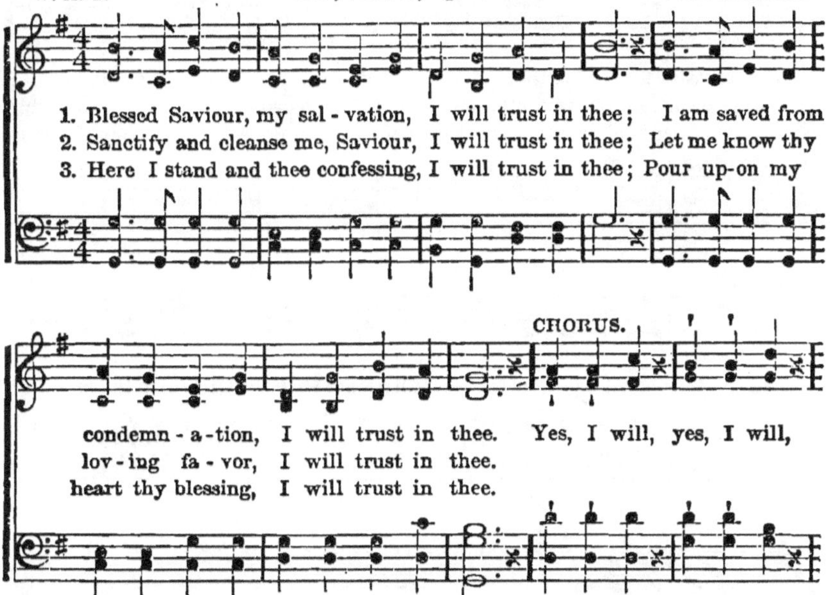

1. Blessed Saviour, my sal-vation, I will trust in thee; I am saved from
2. Sanctify and cleanse me, Saviour, I will trust in thee; Let me know thy
3. Here I stand and thee confessing, I will trust in thee; Pour up-on my

CHORUS.

condemn-a-tion, I will trust in thee. Yes, I will, yes, I will,
lov-ing fa-vor, I will trust in thee.
heart thy blessing, I will trust in thee.

I will trust in thee; Thou, my Strength and Song forever, I will trust in thee.

Copyright, 1886, by JOHN J. HOOD.

116. Meet in the Morning.

H. E. Blair.   Wm. J. Kirkpatrick.

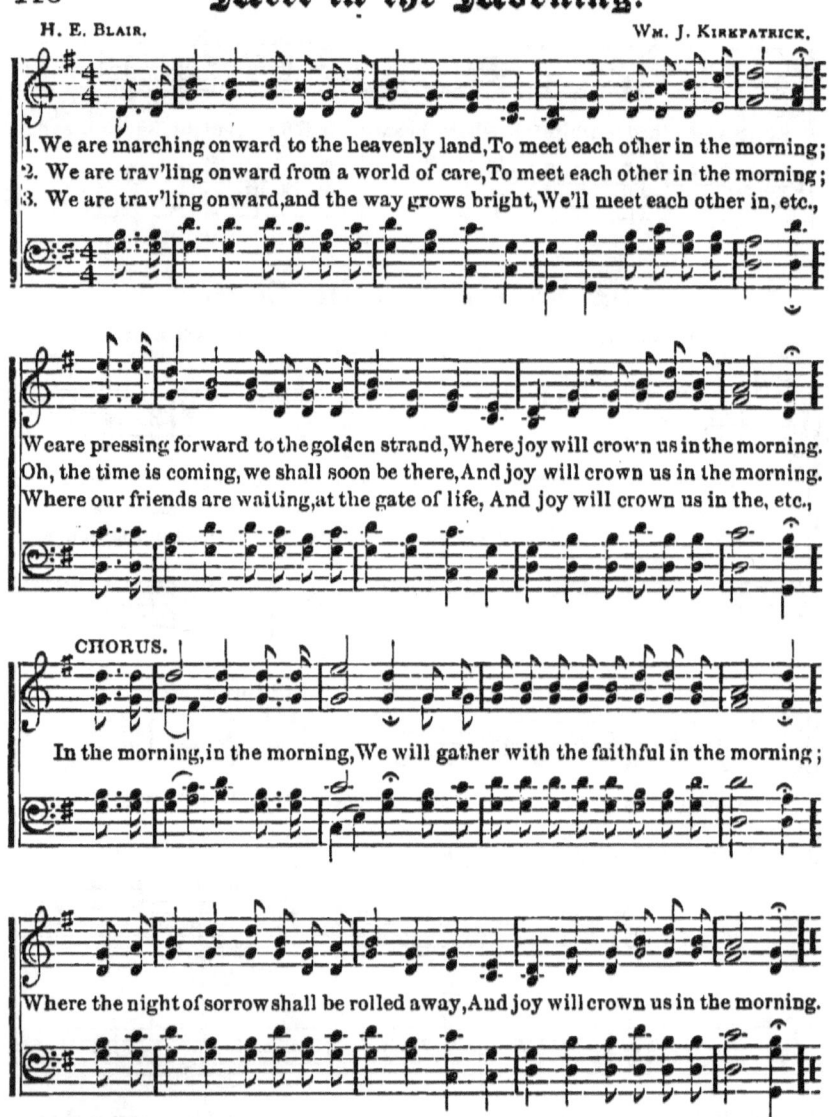

1. We are marching onward to the heavenly land, To meet each other in the morning;
2. We are trav'ling onward from a world of care, To meet each other in the morning;
3. We are trav'ling onward, and the way grows bright, We'll meet each other in, etc.,

We are pressing forward to the golden strand, Where joy will crown us in the morning.
Oh, the time is coming, we shall soon be there, And joy will crown us in the morning.
Where our friends are waiting, at the gate of life, And joy will crown us in the, etc.,

CHORUS.
In the morning, in the morning, We will gather with the faithful in the morning;
Where the night of sorrow shall be rolled away, And joy will crown us in the morning.

4 Where the hills are blooming on the other shore,
We'll meet each other in the morning!
Where the heart's deep longing will be felt no more,
And joy will crown us in the morning.

5 In the boundless rapture of a Saviours' love
We'll meet each other in the morning;
Then we'll sing his glory in the realms above,
And joy will crown us in the morning.

Copyright, 1888, by Wm. J. Kirkpatrick.

We Know Not Why.

SALLIE MARTIN. JNO. R. SWENEY.

4 We know not what our joy will be
When, in the realms of glory,
We at the Saviour's feet shall tell
Redemption's wondrous story.

5 O then, content, we'll walk by faith,
Our hearts his love possessing;
We'll praise him for his mercies past,
And trust for every blessing.

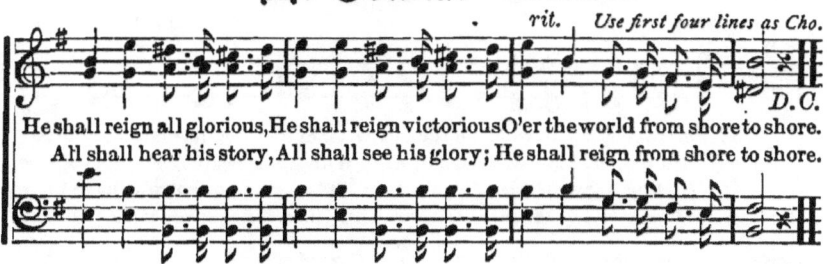

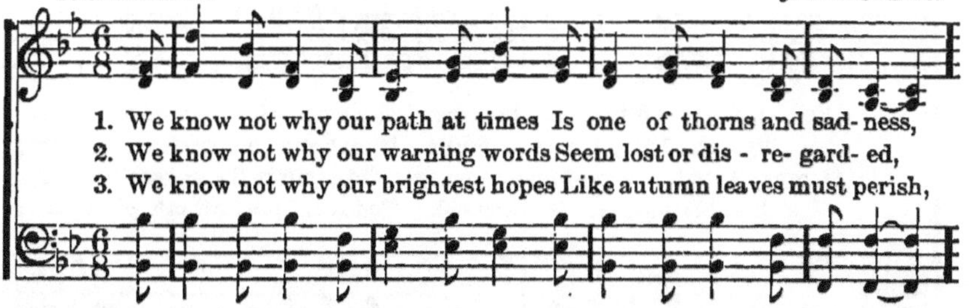

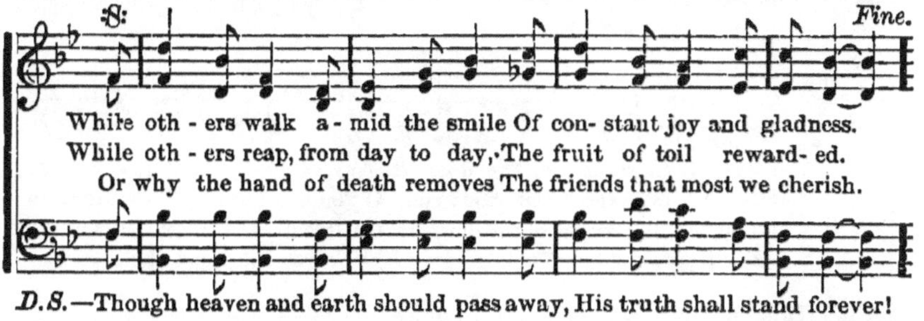

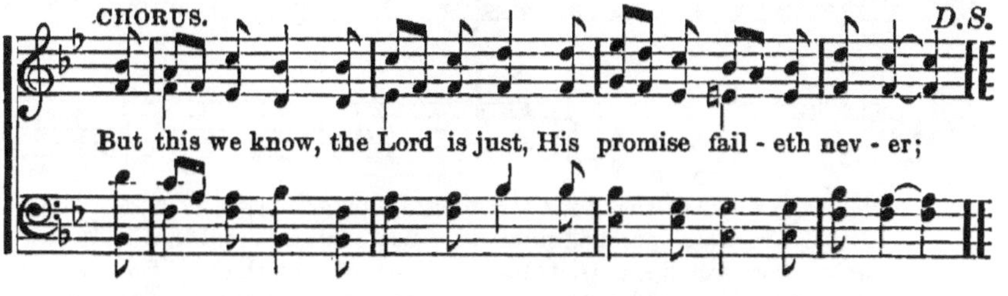

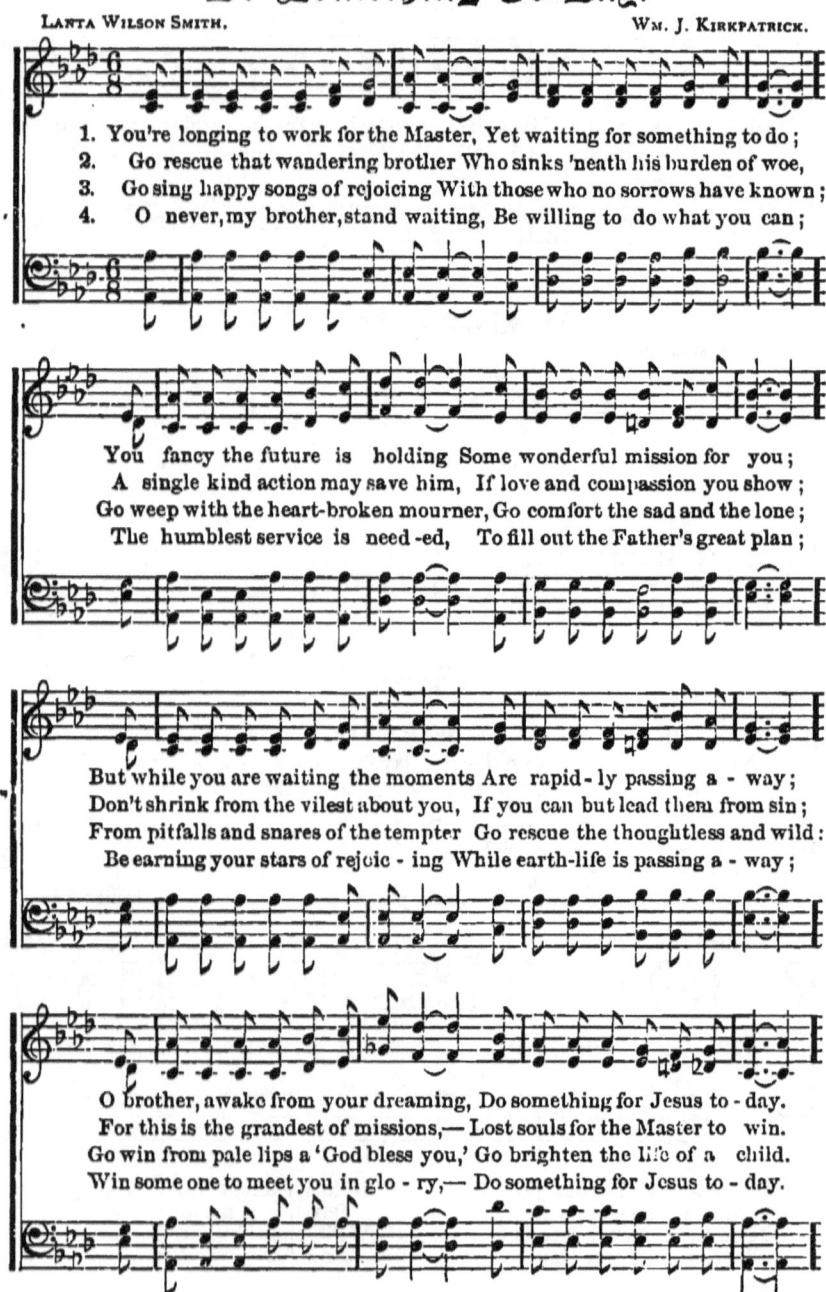

Do Something To-Day.—CONCLUDED

Jesus Will Meet You There.

W. L. K.
W. Lewis Kane.

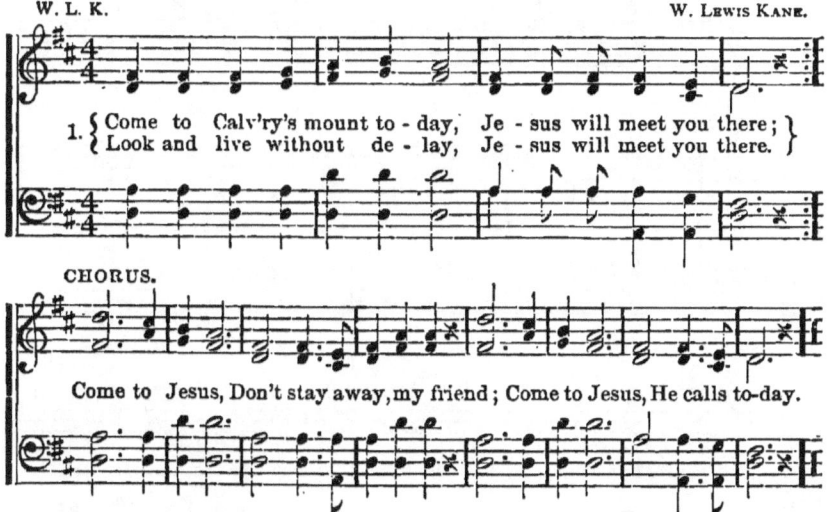

2 Rest beneath the hallowed cross,
    Jesus will meet you there;
  Saving mercy gained for loss,
    Jesus will meet you there.

3 Come and join his faithful band,
    Jesus will meet you there;
  Take his mighty, helping hand,
    Jesus will meet you there.

4 At the blessed mercy seat,
    Jesus will meet you there;
  Come with this assurance sweet,
    Jesus will meet you there.

5 You'll find rest in heaven at last,
    Jesus will meet you there;
  And be happy with the blest,
    Jesus will meet you there.

Copyright, 1888, by Jno. R. Sweney.

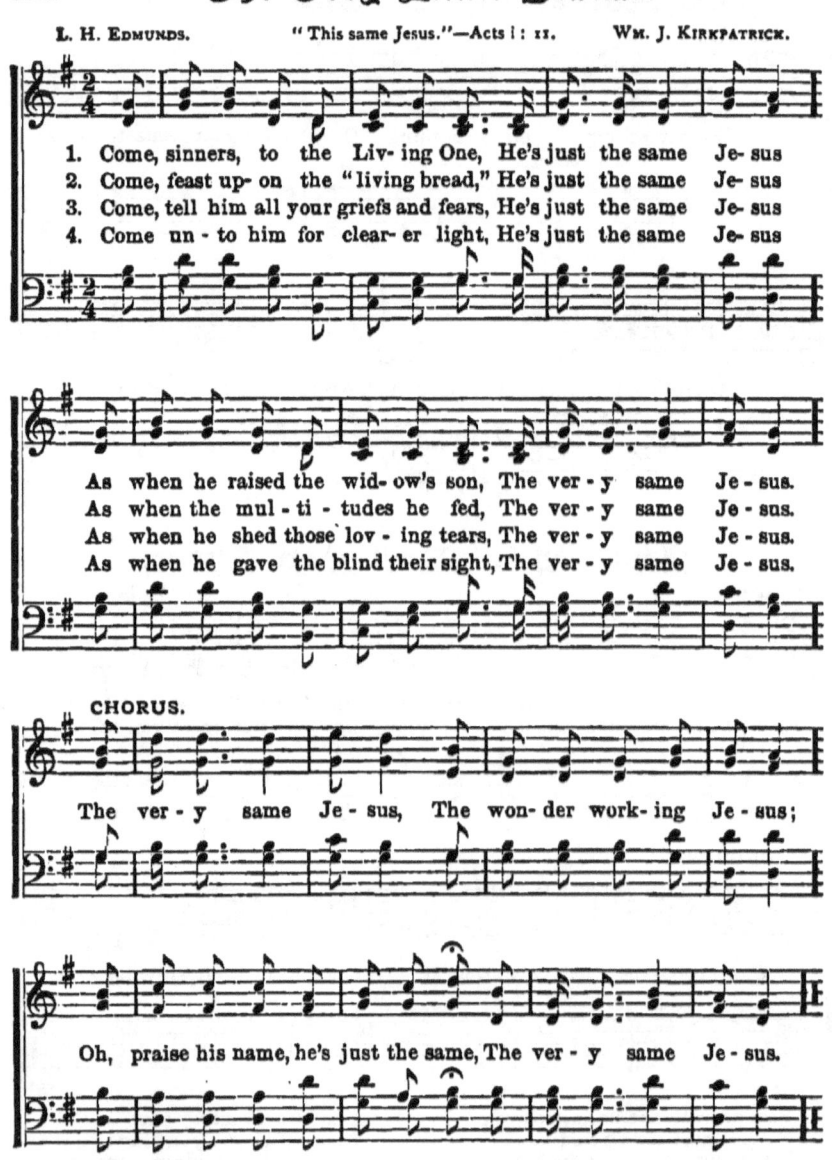

Showers of Blessing. 123

"And I will cause the shower to come down in his season."
Ezekiel xxxiv. 26.

JENNIE GARNETT.   JNO. R. SWENEY.

1. Here in thy name we are gathered, Come and revive us, O Lord;
2. O that the showers of bless-ing Now on our souls may descend,
3. There shall be showers of blessing,—Promise that never can fail;
4. Showers of blessing,—we need them, Showers of blessing from thee;

"There shall be showers of bless-ing" Thou hast declared in thy word.
While at the footstool of mer - cy Pleading thy promise we bend!
Thou wilt regard our pe - ti - tion; Sure - ly our faith will pre - vail.
Showers of blessing,—oh, grant them; Thine all the glory shall be.

CHORUS.

Oh, gracious-ly hear us, Gracious-ly hear us, we pray:
gracious-ly hear us,

Pour from thy windows upon us Showers of blessing to - day.
Lord, pour up - on us

Copyright, 1888, by JNO. R. SWENEY.

Are You Washed in the Blood? 125

E. A. H. — Rev. E. A. Hoffman. By per.

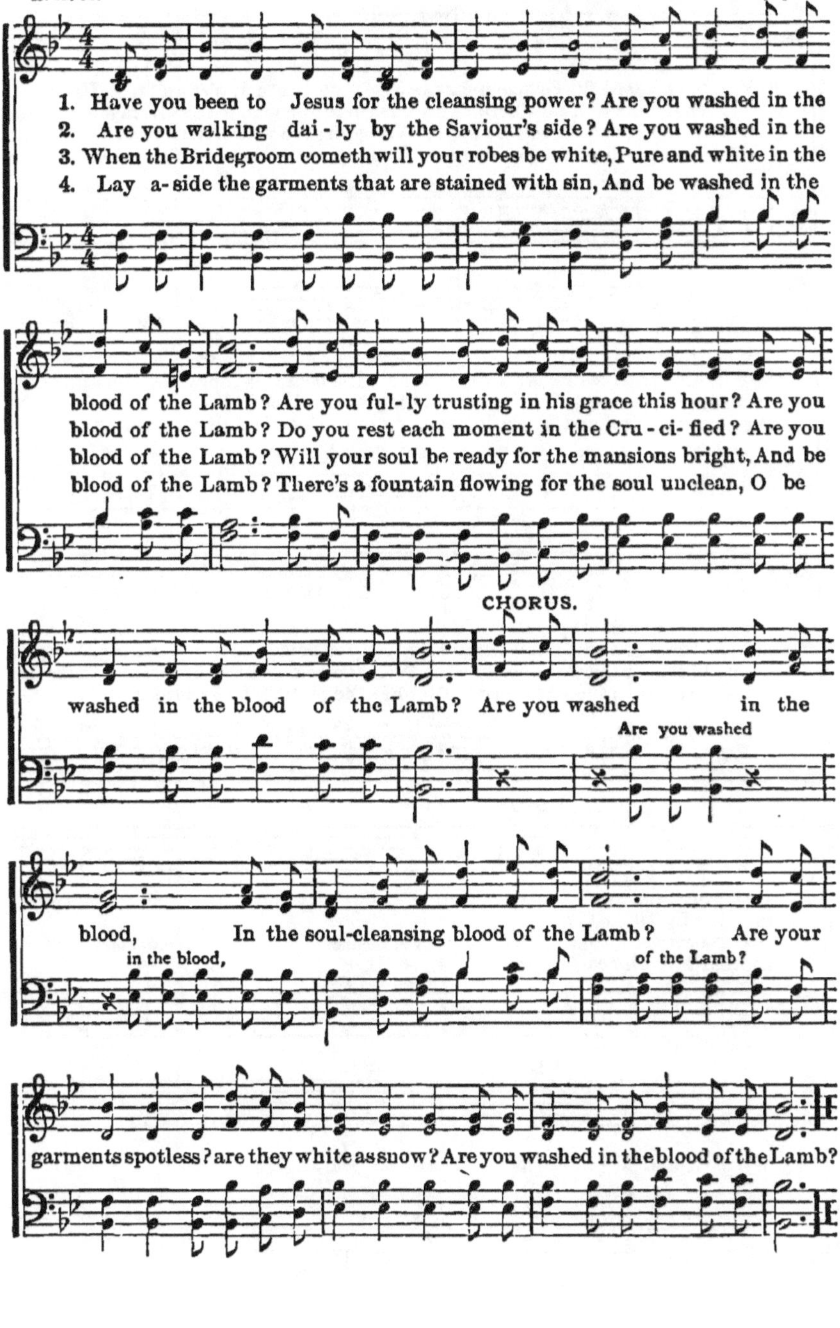
1. Have you been to Jesus for the cleansing power? Are you washed in the
2. Are you walking dai - ly by the Saviour's side? Are you washed in the
3. When the Bridegroom cometh will your robes be white, Pure and white in the
4. Lay a- side the garments that are stained with sin, And be washed in the
blood of the Lamb? Are you ful- ly trusting in his grace this hour? Are you
blood of the Lamb? Do you rest each moment in the Cru - ci- fied? Are you
blood of the Lamb? Will your soul be ready for the mansions bright, And be
blood of the Lamb? There's a fountain flowing for the soul unclean, O be
washed in the blood of the Lamb?
CHORUS.
Are you washed in the blood,
Are you washed
in the blood,
In the soul-cleansing blood of the Lamb?
of the Lamb?
Are your garments spotless? are they white as snow? Are you washed in the blood of the Lamb?

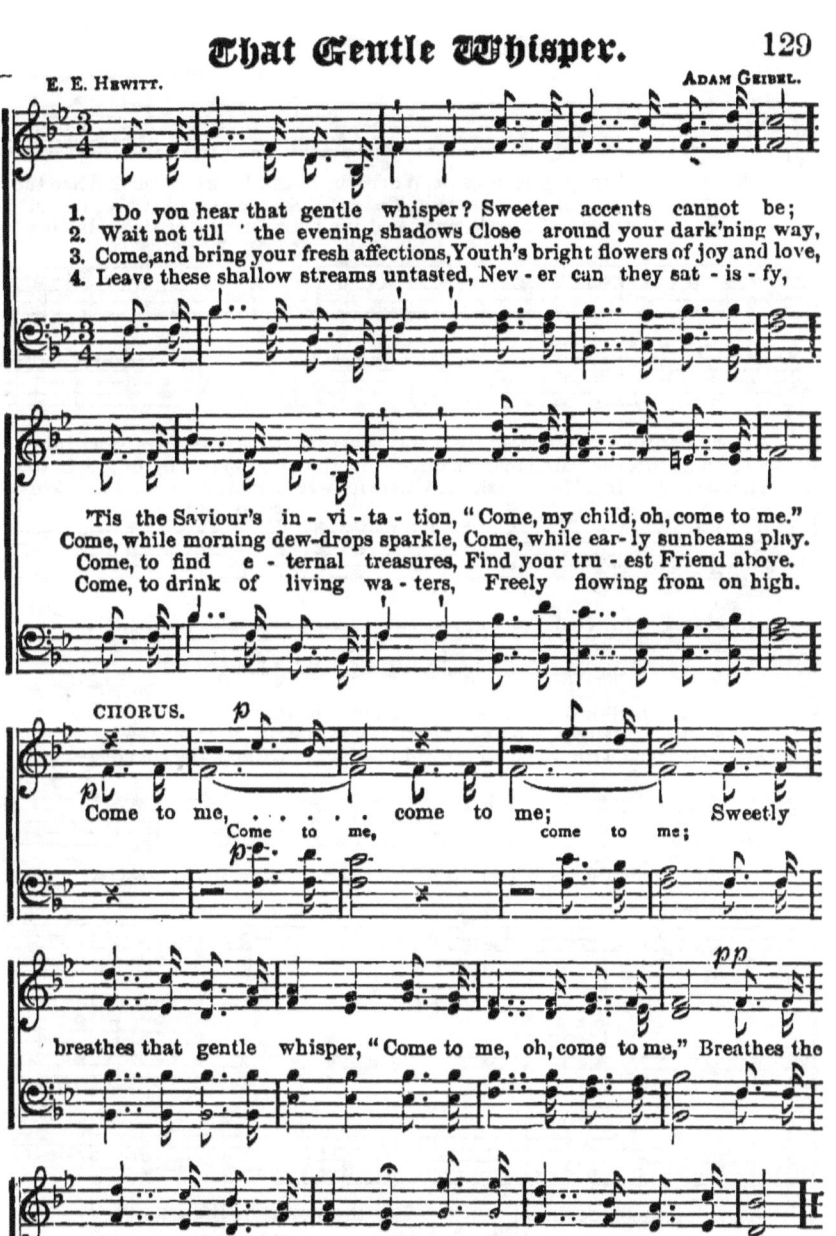

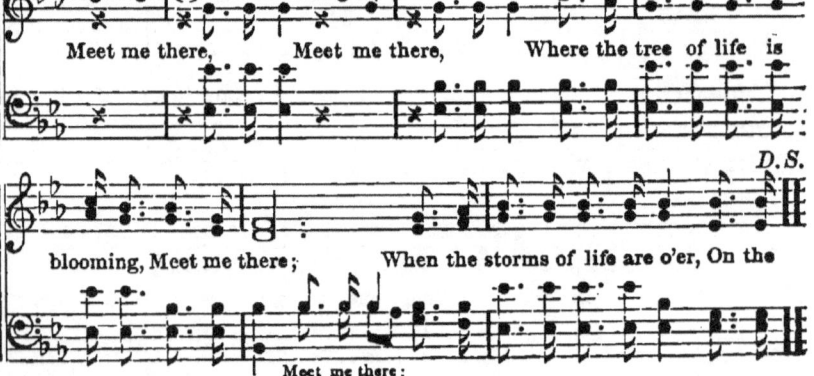

A Shelter in the Time of Storm. 133

Words arranged.   "My God is the Rock of my refuge."—Ps. xciv: 22.   IRA D. SANKEY.

1. The Lord's our Rock, in him we hide, A shelter in the time of storm;
2. A shade by day defence by night, A shelter in the time of storm;
3. The raging storms may round us beat, A shelter in the time of storm;
4. O Rock divine, O Refuge dear, A shelter in the time of storm;

Secure whatev-er ill be-tide, A shelter in the time of storm.
No fears alarm, no foes af-fright, A shelter in the time of storm.
We'll nev-er leave our safe retreat, A shelter in the time of storm.
Be thou our helper ev-er near, A shelter in the time of storm.

CHORUS.

Oh, Jesus is a Rock in a weary land, A weary land, a weary land; Oh, Jesus is a Rock in a weary land, A shelter in the time of storm.

Copyright, 1885, by IRA D. SANKEY.

Only a Beam of Sunshine.—CONCLUDED. 135

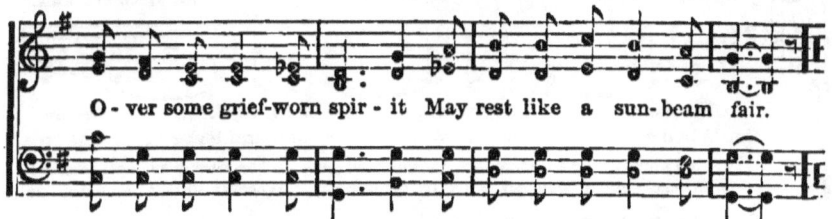

O-ver some grief-worn spir-it May rest like a sun-beam fair.

The New Name.

J. E. H. J. E. HALL.

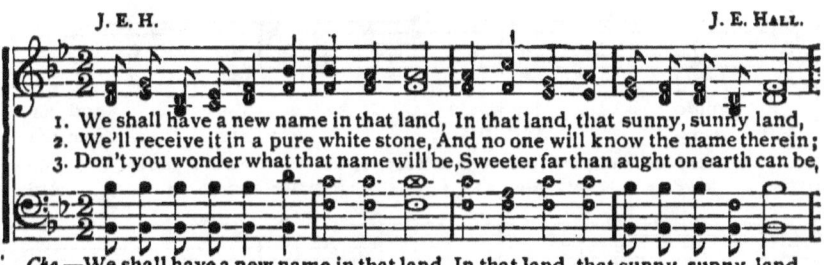

1. We shall have a new name in that land, In that land, that sunny, sunny land,
2. We'll receive it in a pure white stone, And no one will know the name therein;
3. Don't you wonder what that name will be, Sweeter far than aught on earth can be,

Cho.—We shall have a new name in that land, In that land, that sunny, sunny land,

When we meet the bright angelic band, In that sunny land. A new name, a
Only unto him who hath 'tis known, When we're free from sin. A white stone, a
We will be quite satisfied when we Shall that new name know. I won-der, I

When we meet the bright angelic band, In that sunny land.

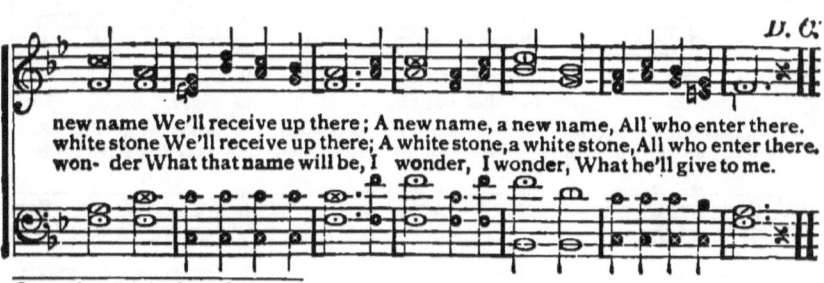

new name We'll receive up there; A new name, a new name, All who enter there.
white stone We'll receive up there; A white stone, a white stone, All who enter there.
won-der What that name will be, I wonder, I wonder, What he'll give to me.

Copyright, 1878, by JOHN J. HOOD.

136. My Shepherd.

Rev. Joseph H. Martin.   Ps. xxiii.   Wm. J. Kirkpatrick.

1. The Lord ... is my shep - - - herd, my keep - - er and guide, ... My wants ... he'll sup- ply, ... and for me .... he'll pro- vide; ... In midst .. of green pas - - - - tures he makes - - me to lie, ... Be-

2. Whenev - - - er I wan - - - der, and leave .. the true way, ... And like ... a lost sheep ... from the flock ... go a - stray; .. My soul ... he re- stores ... to the path ... that is right, ... He

1. The Lord is my shepherd, my keeper and guide, The Lord is my shepherd, my keep- er and guide, My wants he'll supply, and for me he'll provide, My wants he'll sup- ply, and for me he'll provide; In midst of green pastures he makes me to lie, In midst of green pastures he makes me to lie, Be-

2. Whenev-er I wan-der, and leave the true way, When-ev-er I wan-der, and leave the true way, And like a lost sheep from the flock go a-stray, And like a lost sheep from the flock go a-stray; My soul he restores to the path that is right, My soul he restores to the path that is right, He

Copyright, 1880, by John J. Hood.

DO RE MI FA SO LA SI

3 When called to surrender my faltering breath,
And pass through the vale of the shadow of death,
The presence of Jesus will brighten the tomb,
With hope and with gladness dispelling its gloom.
              With gladness dispelling its gloom.

4 For me his free bounty a table has spread;
And blessings unmeasured he pours on my head;
My cup with abundance and joy overflows;
He dries all my tears, and he heals all my woes.
              He heals all my woes, all my woes.

5 His goodness and mercy shall crown all my days,
My mouth shall be filled with thanksgiving and praise;
I'll dwell in his temple of glory above,
And sing evermore of his grace and his love.
              And sing of his grace and his love.

137. Little Ones Like Me.

Jno. R. Sweney.

1. Je-sus, when he left the sky, And for sinners came to die, In his mer-cy passed not by
2. Mothers then the Saviour sought In the places where he taught, And to him the children brought,
3. Did the Saviour say them nay? No, he kindly bade them stay, Suffered none to turn a-way
4. 'Twas for them his life he gave, To redeem them from the grave, Jesus now will gladly save

CHORUS.

Little ones like me. Little ones, little ones,
Little ones like me.
Little ones like me.
Little ones like me.

"Suffer them to come," said he; Jesus loves the little ones, Little ones like me.

Copyright, 1880, by John J. Hood.

138. Touch and Cleanse Me.

Mary F. Marsh.   Matt. viii. 3.   Warren W. Bentley.

1. Touch and cleanse me, blessed Sav-iour, I am wea-ry of my sin;
2. Touch and cleanse me, blessed Sav-iour, Humbly now my guilt I own;
3. Touch and cleanse me, blessed Sav-iour, I am poor, and weak, and blind;
4. Thou dost cleanse me, blessed Sav-iour, Light is streaming from a-bove;

By permission of S. T. Gordon & Son.

Touch and Cleanse Me.—CONCLUDED.

I am long-ing for thy fa - vor, Longing to be pure within.
Oh, be-stow thy pard'ning fa - vor! Thou canst save me, thou alone.
Grant me now thy lov-ing fa - vor, Let me now sal - vation find.
Now I feel thy pard'ning fa - vor, Oh, my soul is full of love.

D.S.—Touch and cleanse me, touch and cleanse me, Jesus, save me or I die.
D.S.—Thou dost cleanse me, thou dost cleanse me, Glory be to God on high.

REFRAIN.

Touch and cleanse me, touch and cleanse me, Listen to my fee-ble cry,
4th v. Thou dost cleanse me, thou dost cleanse me, Thou hast heard my feeble cry,

139 The Morning Light.

SAMUEL F. SMITH.   Tune, WEBB. 7, 6.

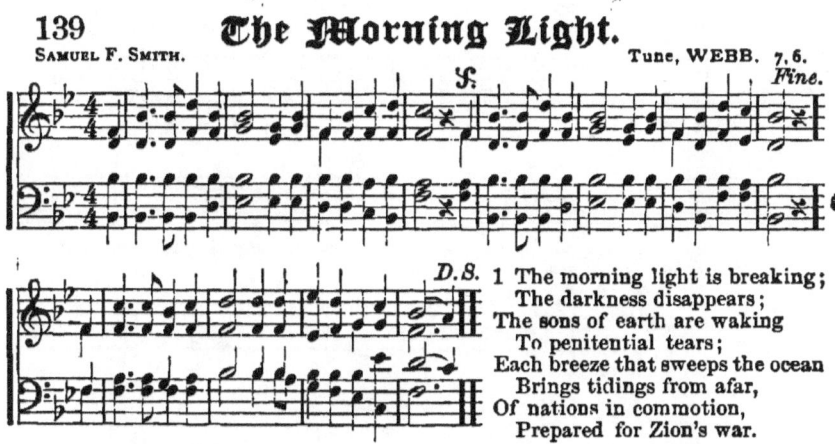

1 The morning light is breaking;
  The darkness disappears;
  The sons of earth are waking
    To penitential tears;
  Each breeze that sweeps the ocean
    Brings tidings from afar,
  Of nations in commotion,
    Prepared for Zion's war.

2 See heathen nations bending
    Before the God we love,
  And thousand hearts ascending
    In gratitude above;
  While sinners, now confessing,
    The gospel call obey,
  And seek the Saviour's blessing,
    A nation in a day.

3 Blest river of salvation,
    Pursue thine onward way;
  Flow thou to every nation,
    Nor in thy richness stay:
  Stay not till all the lowly
    Triumphant reach their home:
  Stay not till all the holy
    Proclaim, "The Lord is come!"

3 Anxious no longer for self,
　Shrinking no longer from pain;
　Leaning on Jesus alone,
　He all my care will sustain.
　Leaning on Jesus, etc.

4 Leaning, I walk in "The Way,"
　Leaning, "The Truth" I shall know;
　Leaning on heart-throbs of Christ,
　Safe into "Life" I may go.
　Leaning on Jesus, etc.

The Firm Foundation.

GEORGE KEITH. Tune, PORTUGUESE HYMN.

1. How firm a foundation, ye saints of the Lord, Is laid for your faith in his excellent word! What more can he say, than to you he hath said, To you, who for refuge to Jesus have fled? To you, who for refuge to Jesus have fled?

2. "Fear not, I am with thee, O be not dismayed, For I am thy God, I will still give thee aid; I'll strengthen thee, help thee, and cause thee to stand, Upheld by my gracious, omnipotent hand, Upheld by my gracious, omnipotent hand.

3. "When thro' the deep waters I call thee to go, The rivers of sorrow shall not overflow; For I will be with thee thy trials to bless, And sanctify to thee thy deepest distress, And sanctify to thee thy deepest distress.

4. "When thro' fiery trials thy pathway shall lie, My grace all sufficient, shall be thy supply, The flame shall not hurt thee; I only design Thy dross to consume, and thy gold to refine, Thy dross to consume, and thy gold to refine.

5 " E'en down to old age all my people shall prove [love,
My sovereign, eternal, unchangeable
And when hoary hairs shall their temples adorn, [be borne.
Like lambs they shall still in my bosom

6 " The soul that on Jesus hath leaned for repose,
I will not, I will not desert to his foes;
That soul, though all hell should endeavor to shake,
I'll never, no never, no never forsake!"

Redeemed, Praise the Lord.

ABBIE MILLS.   WM. J. KIRKPATRICK.

1. O happy day! what a Sav-iour is mine! I am redeemed, praise the Lord!
2. O clap your hands, all ye people of God, I am redeemed, praise the Lord!
3. Thanks be to God for the great vict'ry given, I am redeemed, praise the Lord!
4. Glory to God, I would shout ev-ermore, I am redeemed, praise the Lord!

Fine.

All to his pleasure I glad-ly re-sign, I am redeemed, praise the Lord!
Let ev'ry tongue speak his mercy abroad, I am redeemed, praise the Lord!
Now I am free; ev'ry chain has been riven,—I am redeemed, praise the Lord!
O for a voice that could reach ev'ry shore, I am redeemed, praise the Lord!

Key C.

Jesus has taken my burden away; Jesus has turned all my night into day;
His loving-kindness is better than gold; He doth bestow more than my cup can hold;
Out of the pit, and the mire, and the clay, Jesus has borne me in triumph away;
Help me, ye ransom'd, awake, ev'ry string, Let earth rejoice and the whole heavens ring,

Use first four lines as Chorus. D.C.

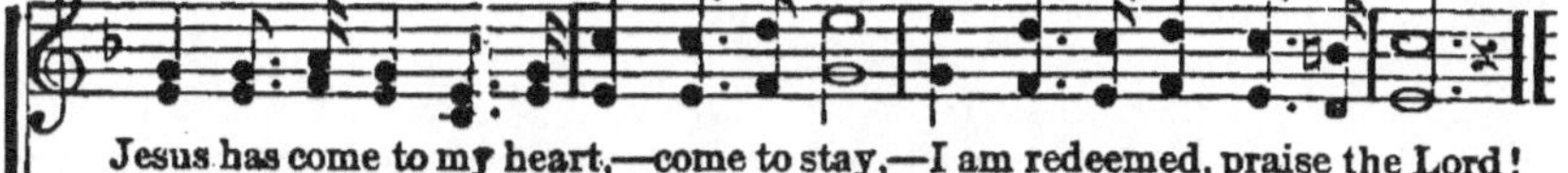

Jesus has come to my heart,—come to stay,—I am redeemed, praise the Lord!
Wondrous Salvation, that ne'er can be told,—I am redeemed, praise the Lord!
Safe on the rock I am standing to-day,—I am redeemed, praise the Lord!
While we the chorus u-ni-ted-ly sing, I am redeemed, praise the Lord!

Copyright, 1896, by JOHN J. HOOD.   *Temple Songs—K*

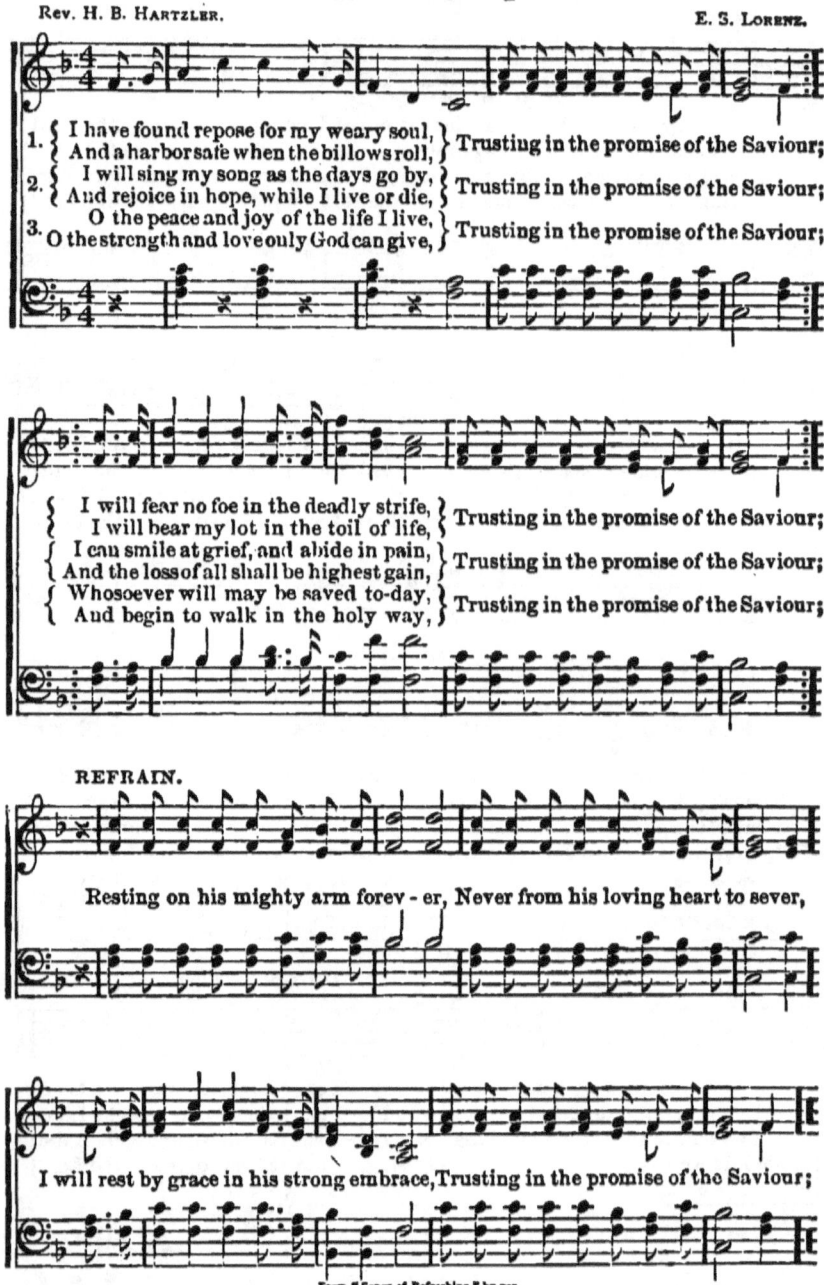

Come to Jesus. 147

J. H. S.   Rev. J. H. Stockton.

1. Come, ev-'ry soul by sin oppressed, There's mercy with the Lord;
2. For Jesus shed his precious blood Rich blessings to bestow;
3. Yes, Jesus is the Truth, the Way, That leads you in-to rest;

And he will surely give you rest, By trusting in his word.
Plunge now in-to the crimson flood That washes white as snow.
Believe in him, without delay, And you are fully blest.

D. S.—He will save you, he will save you, He will save you now.

CHORUS.   *D. S.*

Come to Jesus, come to Jesus, Come to Jesus now!
Second Chorus.
Only trust him, only trust him, Only trust him now;

4 O Jesus, blessed Jesus, dear,
   I'm coming now to thee;
Since thou hast made the way so clear,
   And full salvation free.

5 Come, then, and join this holy band,
   And on to glory go;
To dwell in that celestial land
   Where joys immortal flow.

By permission.

Come, Humble Sinner.   Tune above.

1 Come, humble sinner, in whose breast
   A thousand thoughts revolve,
Come, with your guilt and fear opprest,
   And make this last resolve:—

2 I'll go to Jesus, though my sin
   Like mountains round me close;
I know his courts, I'll enter in,
   Whatever may oppose.

3 Prostrate I'll lie before his throne,
   And there my guilt confess;
I'll tell him I'm a wretch undone,
   Without his sovereign grace.

4 Perhaps he will admit my plea,
   Perhaps will hear my prayer;
But, if I perish, I will pray,
   And perish only there.

5 I can but perish, if I go;
   I am resolved to try:
For if I stay away I know
   I must forever die. —Edmund Jones.

151. I am Coming to the Cross.

Rev. Wm. McDonald. — John vi. 37. — Wm. G. Fischer. By per.

1. I am com-ing to the cross; I am poor, and weak, and blind;
2. Long my heart has sighed for thee, Long has e - vil reigned within;
3. Here I give my all to thee, Friends, and time, and earthly store;

Cho.—I am trust-ing, Lord, in thee, Blest Lamb of Cal-va-ry;
D.C.

I am count-ing all but dross, I shall full sal-va-tion find.
Je-sus sweet-ly speaks to me,— "I will cleanse you from all sin."
Soul and bo-dy thine to be,—Whol-ly thine for ev-er-more.

Humbly at thy cross I bow, Save me, Je-sus, save me now.

4 In thy promises I trust,
Now I feel the blood applied:
I am prostrate in the dust,
I with Christ am crucified.

5 Jesus comes! he fills my soul!
Perfected in him I am;
I am every whit made whole:
Glory, glory to the Lamb.

152. Rest for the Weary.

Rev. S. G. Harmer. — Rev. Wm. McDonald.

1. In the Christian's home in glo-ry There re-mains a land of rest;
2. Pain or sickness ne'er shall en-ter, Grief nor woe my lot shall share;
3. Death itself shall then be vanquished, And his sting shall be withdrawn;
4. Sing, oh, sing, ye heirs of glo-ry; Shout your triumph as you go;

There my Saviour's gone be-fore me, To ful - fil my soul's request.
But in that ce-les-tial cen-tre, I a crown of life shall wear.
Shout for gladness, O ye ransomed! Hail with joy the ris-ing morn.
Zi-on's gates will o-pen for you, You shall find an entrance through.

CHORUS.

{ There is rest for the wea-ry, There is rest for the
{ On the oth-er side of Jor-dan, In the sweet fields of

wea-ry, There is rest for the wea-ry, There is rest for you—
E-den, Where the tree of life is blooming, There is rest for you.

153. Come, Ye Disconsolate.

THOMAS MOORE, alt., and THOS. HASTINGS. SAMUEL WEBBE.

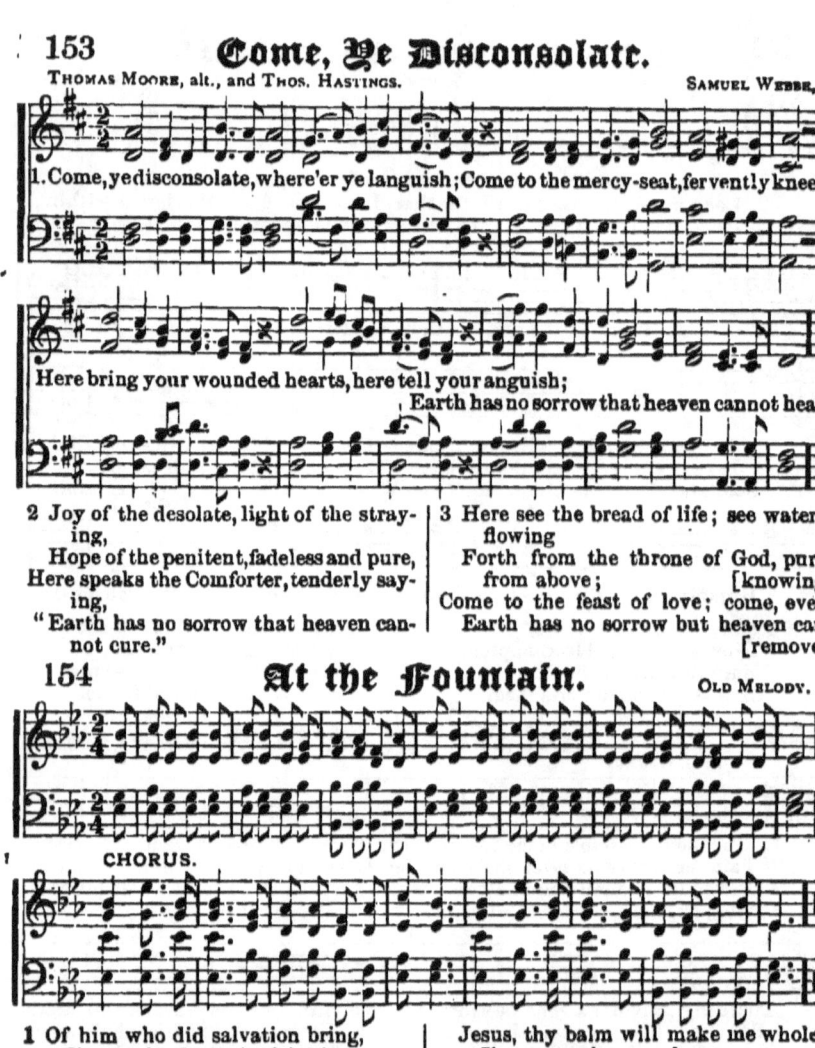

1. Come, ye disconsolate, where'er ye languish; Come to the mercy-seat, fervently kneel; Here bring your wounded hearts, here tell your anguish; Earth has no sorrow that heaven cannot heal.

2 Joy of the desolate, light of the straying,
  Hope of the penitent, fadeless and pure,
Here speaks the Comforter, tenderly saying,
  "Earth has no sorrow that heaven cannot cure."

3 Here see the bread of life; see waters flowing
  Forth from the throne of God, pure from above; [knowing
Come to the feast of love; come, ever
Earth has no sorrow but heaven can [remove.

154. At the Fountain.

OLD MELODY.

CHORUS.

1 Of him who did salvation bring,
  I'm at the fountain drinking,
I could forever think and sing,
  I'm on my journey home.
  CHO.—Glory to God,
    I'm at the fountain drinking,
    Glory to God,
    I'm on my journey home.

2 Ask but his grace and lo! 'tis given,
  I'm at the fountain drinking,
Ask and he turns your hell to heaven,
  I'm on my journey home.

3 Tho' sin and sorrow wound my soul,
  I'm at the fountain drinking,
Jesus, thy balm will make me whole,
  I'm on my journey home.

4 Where'er I am, where'er I move,
  I'm at the fountain drinking,
I meet the object of my love,
  I'm on my journey home.

5 Insatiate to this spring I fly,
  I'm at the fountain drinking,
I drink and yet am ever dry,
  I'm on my journey home.
  CHO.—Glory to God,
    I'm at the fountain drinking,
    Glory to God,
    My soul is satisfied.

155 We'll Work till Jesus Comes.

Mrs. Elizabeth Mills.   Arr. by W. J. K., 1859.   Dr. Wm. Miller.

1 O land of rest for thee I sigh,
  When will the moment come,
  When I shall lay my armor by
  And dwell in peace at home?

Cho.—We'll work till Jesus comes,
  We'll work till Jesus comes,
  We'll work till Jesus comes,
  And we'll be gather'd home.

2 No tranquil joys on earth I know,
  No peaceful sheltering dome,
  This world's a wilderness of woe,
  This world is not my home.

3 To Jesus Christ I fled for rest;
  He bade me cease to roam,
  And lean for succor on his breast
  Till he conduct me home.

4 I sought at once my Saviour's side,
  No more my steps shall roam;
  With him I'll brave death's chilling tide,
  And reach my heavenly home.

156 Happy Land.

Old Melody.

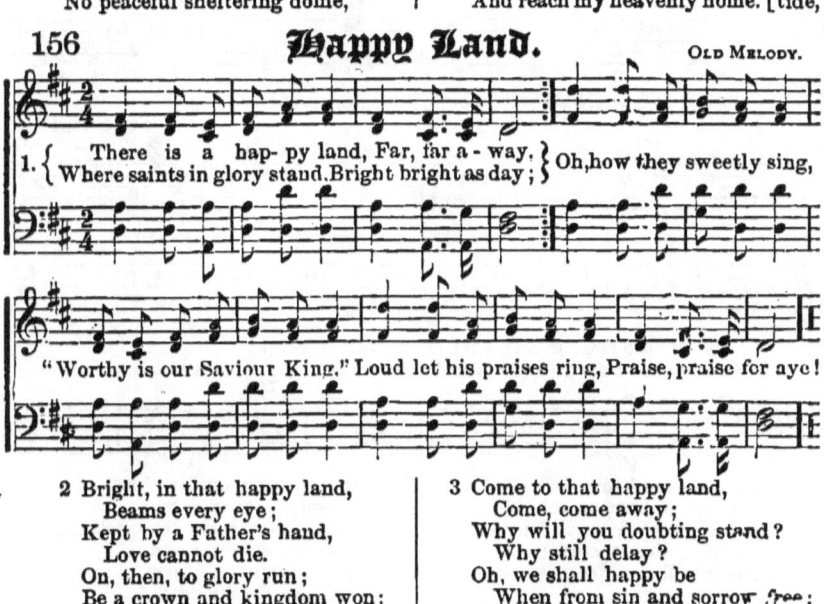

1. There is a happy land, Far, far away,
   Where saints in glory stand, Bright, bright as day;
   Oh, how they sweetly sing,
   "Worthy is our Saviour King." Loud let his praises ring, Praise, praise for aye!

2 Bright, in that happy land,
  Beams every eye;
  Kept by a Father's hand,
  Love cannot die.
  On, then, to glory run;
  Be a crown and kingdom won;
  And bright, above the sun,
  Reign evermore.

3 Come to that happy land,
  Come, come away;
  Why will you doubting stand?
  Why still delay?
  Oh, we shall happy be
  When from sin and sorrow free;
  Lord, we shall dwell with thee,
  Blest evermore.

157. Will You Go?

1 We're trav'ling home to heaven above,
　　Will you go?
To sing the Saviour's dying love;
　　Will you go?
Millions have reached that blest abode,
Anointed kings and priests to God;
And millions more are on the road;
　　Will you go?

2 We're going to walk the plains of light,
　　Will you go?
Far, far from curse and death and night;
　　Will you go?
The crown of life we then shall wear,
The conqueror's palm we then shall bear,
And all the joys of heaven we'll share;
　　Will you go?

3 The way to heaven is straight and plain;
　　Will you go?
Repent, believe, be born again;
　　Will you go?
The Saviour cries aloud to thee,
"Take up your cross and follow me,
And thou shalt my salvation see."
　　Will you go?

158. While Jesus Whispers to You.

WILL. E. WITTER.　　　　　　　　　H. R. PALMER.

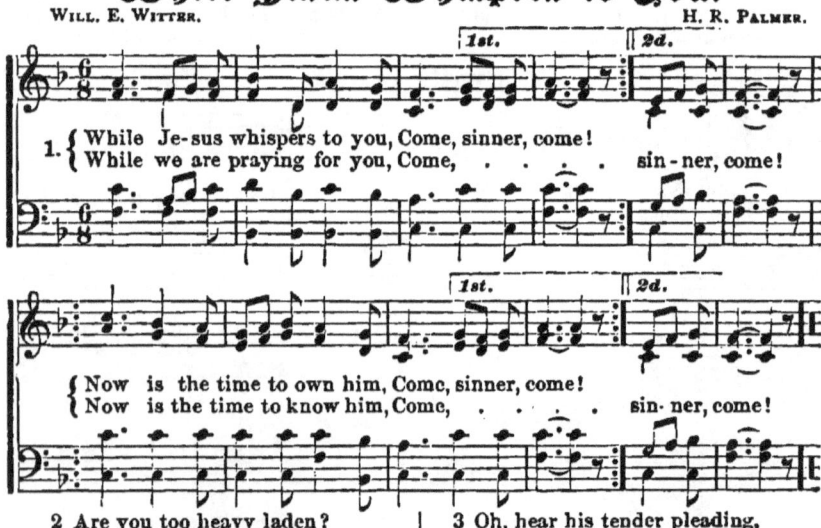

2 Are you too heavy laden?
　　Come, sinner, come!
Jesus will bear your burden,
　　Come, sinner, come!
Jesus will not deceive you,
　　Come, sinner, come!
Jesus can now redeem you,
　　Come, sinner, come!

3 Oh, hear his tender pleading,
　　Come, sinner, come!
Come and receive the blessing,
　　Come, sinner, come!
While Jesus whispers to you,
　　Come, sinner, come!
While we are praying for you,
　　Come, sinner, come!

Copyright, 1879, by H. R. Palmer.

159 Crown Him.

"Thou hast crowned him with glory and honor."
Psalm viii. 5.

Rev. Thos. Kelly. Arr. by Geo. G. Stebbins. By per 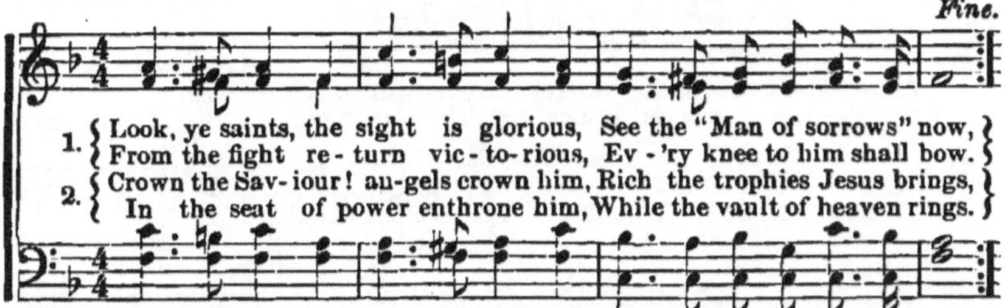
Fine.

1. Look, ye saints, the sight is glorious, See the "Man of sorrows" now,
   From the fight return victorious, Ev-'ry knee to him shall bow.
2. Crown the Sav-iour! an-gels crown him, Rich the trophies Jesus brings,
   In the seat of power enthrone him, While the vault of heaven rings.

D. C.—Crown him! crown him, angels crown him! Crown the Saviour King of kings.

REFRAIN. *D. C.*

Crown him! crown him, angels crown him! Crown the Saviour King of kings;

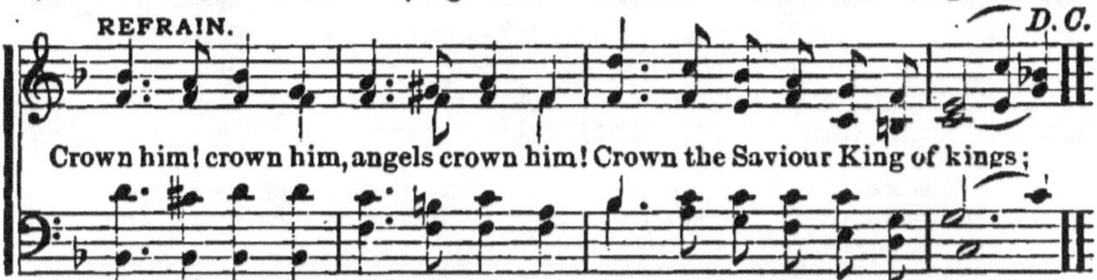

3 Sinners in derision crowned him,
  Mocking thus the Saviour's claim,
  Saints and angels crowd around him,
  Own his title, praise his name.

4 Hark! the bursts of acclamation!
  Hark! these loud, triumphant chords,
  Jesus takes the highest station,
  Oh, what joy the sight affords!

160 My Faith Looks Up to Thee.

Ray Palmer. L. Mason.

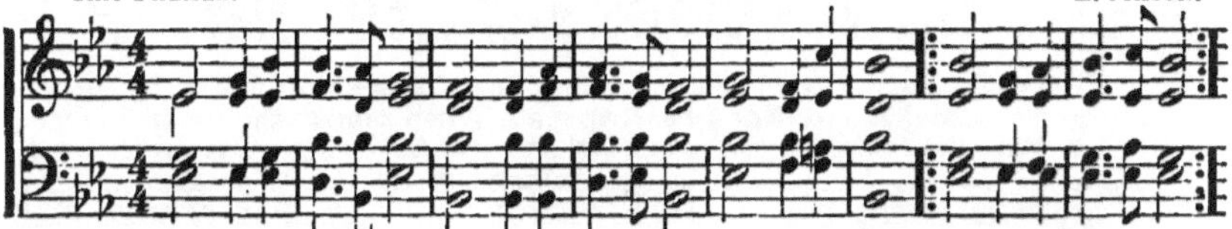

1 My faith looks up to thee,
  Thou Lamb of Calvary,
   Saviour divine!
  Now hear me while I pray;
  Take all my guilt away;
  Oh, let me from this day
   Be wholly thine!

2 May thy rich grace impart
  Strength to my fainting heart,
   My zeal inspire!
  As thou hast died for me,
  Oh, may my love to thee
  Pure, warm, amd changeless be—
   A living fire!

3 While life's dark maze I tread,
  And griefs around me spread,
   Be thou my guide;
  Bid darkness turn to day,
  Wipe sorrow's tears away,
  Nor let me ever stray
   From thee aside.

4 When ends life's transient dream,
  When death's cold sullen stream
   Shall o'er me roll,
  Blest Saviour! then, in love,
  Fear and distrust remove;
  Oh, bear me safe above—
   A ransomed soul!

161. He is Calling.

FABER.   Arr. by S. J. VAIL.

1. There's a wideness in God's mercy, Like the wideness of the sea:
There's a kindness in his justice Which is more than li-ber-ty.

CHORUS.
He is call-ing, "Come to me!" Lord, I'll gladly haste to thee.

2. There is welcome for the sinner,
And more graces for the good;
There is mercy with the Saviour;
There is healing in his blood.

3. For the love of God is broader
Than the measure of man's mind;

And the heart of the Eternal
Is most wonderful and kind.

4. If our love were but more simple,
We should take him at his word;
And our lives would be all sunshine
In the sweetness of our Lord.

162. The Golden Key.

"Prayer is the key to unlock the door, and the bolt to shut in the night."   J. R. S.

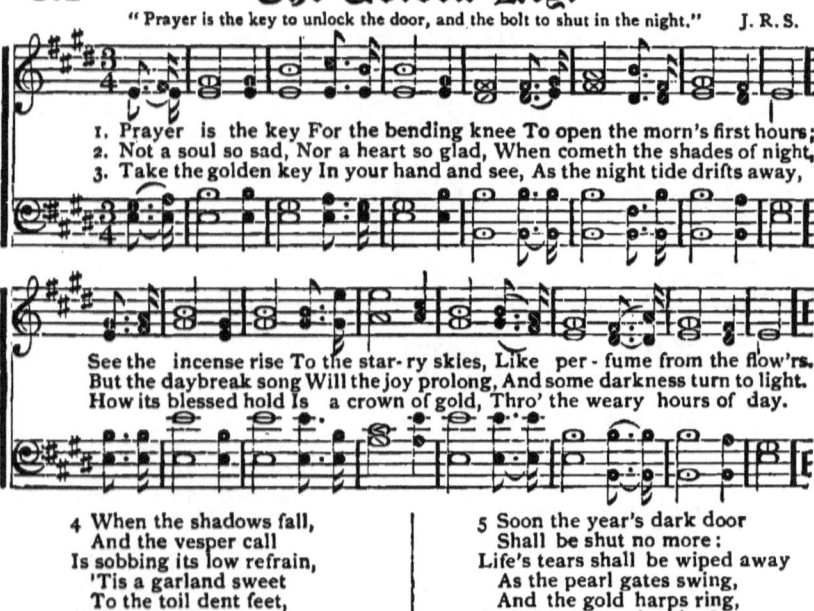

1. Prayer is the key For the bending knee To open the morn's first hours;
2. Not a soul so sad, Nor a heart so glad, When cometh the shades of night,
3. Take the golden key In your hand and see, As the night tide drifts away,

See the incense rise To the star-ry skies, Like per-fume from the flow'rs.
But the daybreak song Will the joy prolong, And some darkness turn to light.
How its blessed hold Is a crown of gold, Thro' the weary hours of day.

4 When the shadows fall,
And the vesper call
Is sobbing its low refrain,
'Tis a garland sweet
To the toil dent feet,
And an antidote for pain.

5 Soon the year's dark door
Shall be shut no more:
Life's tears shall be wiped away
As the pearl gates swing,
And the gold harps ring,
And the sun unsheathe for aye.

From "Goodly Pearls," by per.

163 Cleansing Wave.

Mrs. J. F. KNAPP.

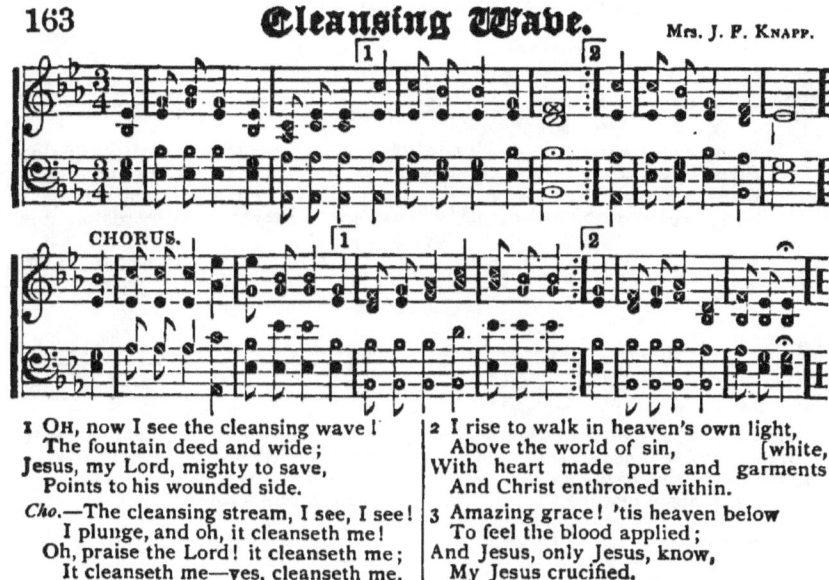

1 OH, now I see the cleansing wave!
  The fountain deep and wide;
Jesus, my Lord, mighty to save,
  Points to his wounded side.

Cho.—The cleansing stream, I see, I see!
  I plunge, and oh, it cleanseth me!
Oh, praise the Lord! it cleanseth me;
  It cleanseth me—yes, cleanseth me.

2 I rise to walk in heaven's own light,
  Above the world of sin, [white,
With heart made pure and garments
  And Christ enthroned within.

3 Amazing grace! 'tis heaven below
  To feel the blood applied;
And Jesus, only Jesus, know,
  My Jesus crucified.

164 Doxology.

Words arr. by B. M. A.   Melody by J. R. S.   Harmony by W. J. K.

Slow, with dignity.

Glo - ry be to the FA - THER, Glo - ry be to the SON,
Glo - ry be to the HO - LY GHOST; As it was in the be - ginning,
Is now, and ev - er shall be, World without end. A - men, a - men.

167 But the Lord is Mindful of His Own.

From the "Oratorio of St. Paul."   MENDELSSOHN.

Recitative.

And he journey'd with companions towards Damascus, and had authority and command from the High Priest, that he might bring them bound, men and women, unto Jerusalem.

Arioso.—Andantino.

But the Lord is mindful of his own, he remembers his children, But the

ritard.

Lord is mindful of his own, the Lord remembers his children, re-

mem - - bers his children.

Off S. D.

But the Lord is Mindful.—CONCLUDED. 168

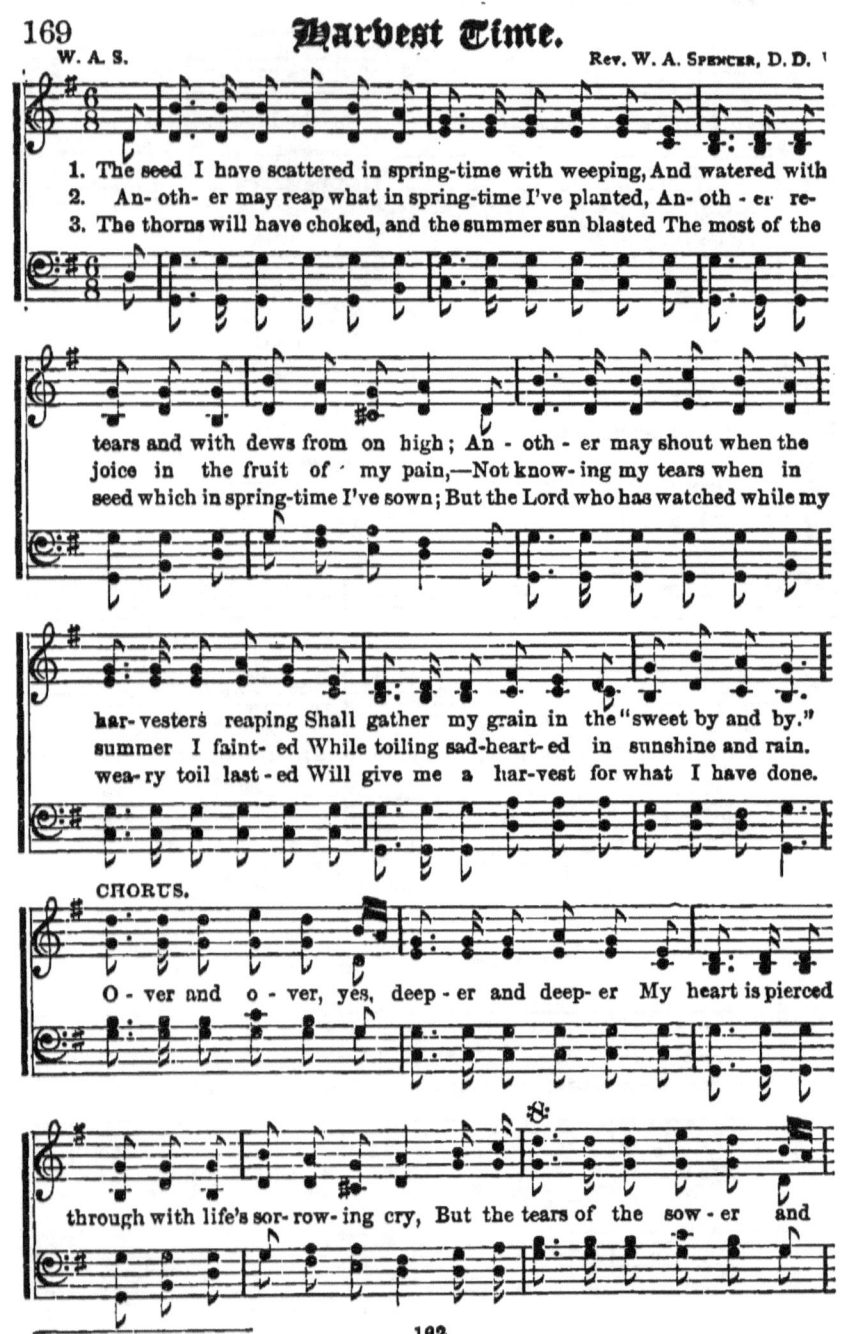

Harvest Time.—CONCLUDED.

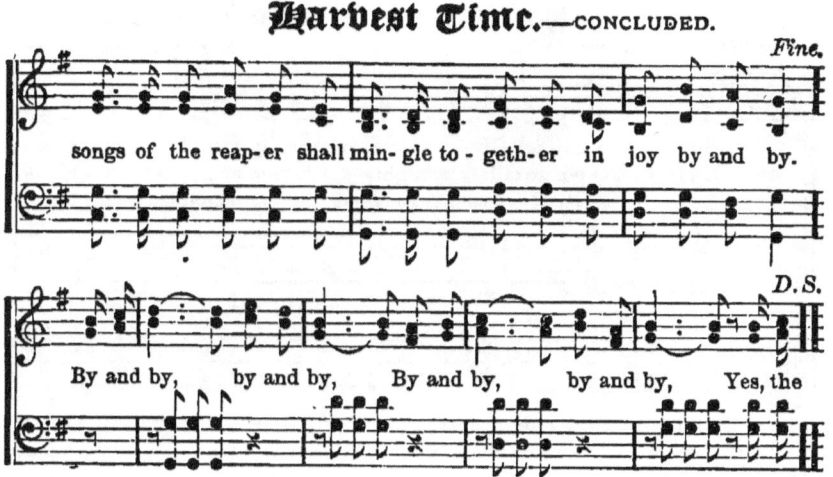

170. Saviour, Pilot Me.
J. E. GOULD.

1 Jesus, Saviour, pilot me
  Over life's tempestuous sea;
  Unknown waves before me roll,
  Hiding rock and treacherous shoal;
  Chart and compass came from thee:
  Jesus, Saviour, pilot me.

2 When the Apostles' fragile bark
  Struggled with the billows dark,
  On the stormy Galilee,
  Thou did'st walk across the sea;
  And when they beheld thy form,
  Safe they glided through the storm.

3 As a mother stills her child
  Thou canst hush the ocean wild;
  Boisterous waves obey thy will
  When thou say'st to them "Be still."
  Wondrous Sovereign of the sea,
  Jesus, Saviour, pilot me.

4 When at last I near the shore,
  And the fearful breakers roar
  'Twixt me and the peaceful rest,
  Then, while leaning on thy breast,
  May I hear thee say to me,
  "Fear not, I will pilot thee."

172. Why Don't You Come?

L. W. Munhall.   C. R. Dunbar. By per.

1. O ye wand'rers, come to Jesus, He is calling you to-day;
2. You are needy, lost, and weary; You are sick and wounded sore;
3. Do not think your works have merit, Cast your deadly goodness down
4. Do not wait until you're better, For you surely will be lost;

By his sovereign grace he frees us: Come, be saved while now you may.
Long have trod the way most dreary; Can you ever need him more?
Not by these can you inherit Life eternal—heaven's crown.
Come, he'll break sin's ev'ry fetter; Come, at once, at any cost.

REFRAIN.

Why don't you come to Jesus? He's waiting to receive you, Why don't you come to Jesus and be saved? saved?

5 He from heaven came to save you,
   Hung upon th'-accursed tree,
'Rose from death to justify you,
   Waits to intercede for thee.

6 Yield just now, in glad submission,
   In repentance, faith, and love;
He will grant you full remission,
   Take you to his home above.

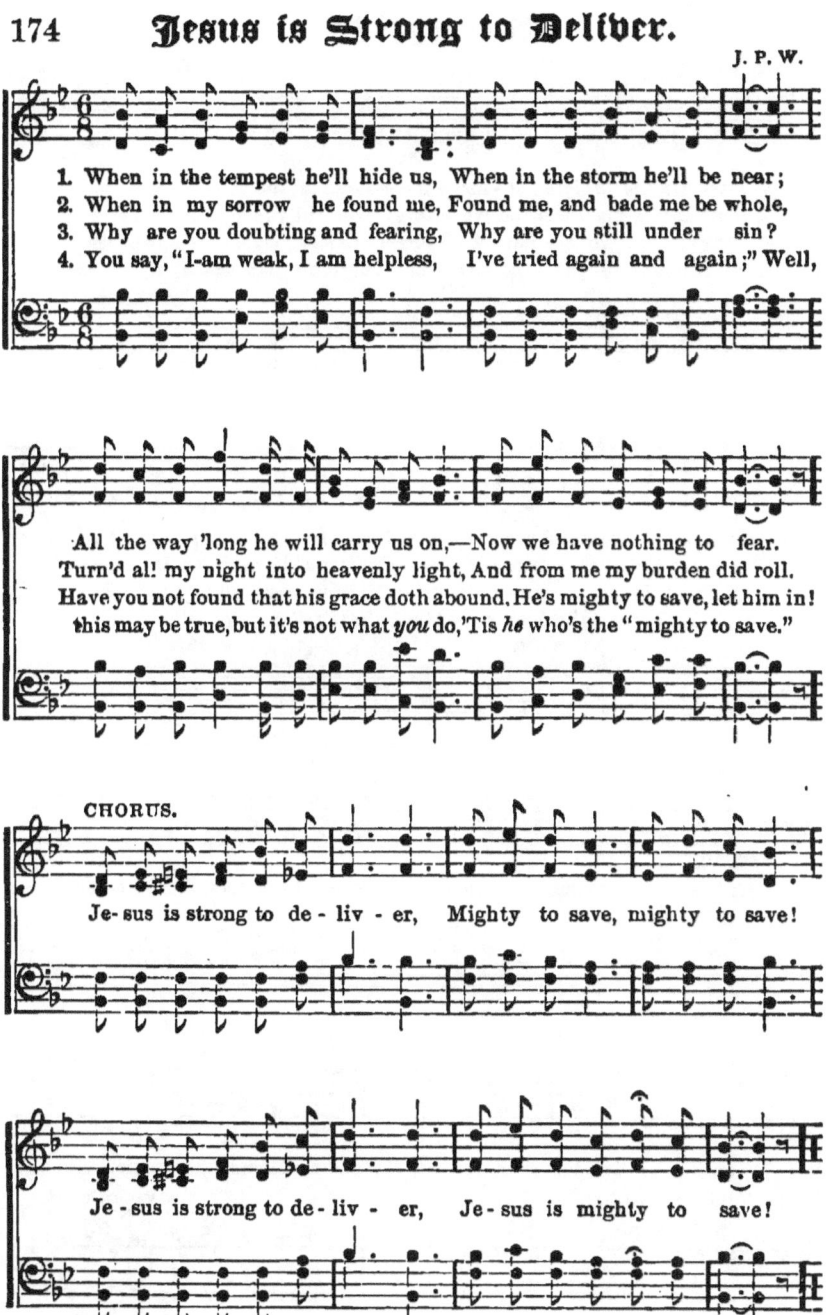

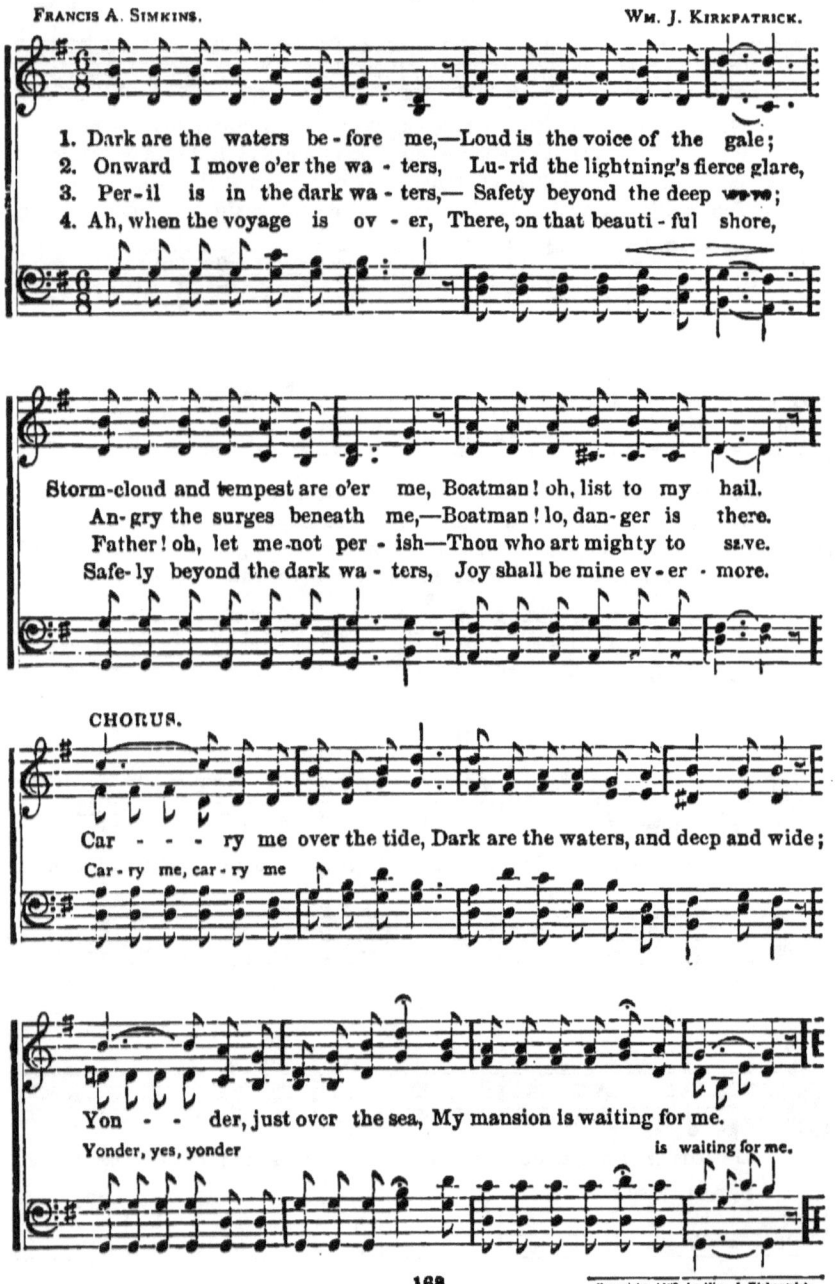

177. Going away Unsaved.

"Ye will not come to me that ye might have life." — JOHN v: 40.

Words arranged.   D. B. TOWNER. By per.

1. Some go a-way from the house to-night, Pu-ri-fied from sin,
2. Some go a-way from the house of God, Filled with joy and peace,
3. Some go a-way from the house to-night, Bow'd with guilt and shame,

Others re-ject the gracious light, And go a-way un-clean;
Others de-spise the precious blood That brings the soul re-lease.
Others re-ceiv-ing life and light, Con-fess the Saviour's name;

Lov-ing-ly still the Saviour stands, Pleading with thy heart,
Nev-er a-gain the Saviour dear May be of-fered thee,
Hap-py are they who share his grace, Trusting in his word;

Fine.

Patient-ly knocks with bleeding hands, Un-wil-ling to de-part.
Nev-er a-gain thy soul may hear The Spir-it's ten-der plea.
Give him thy heart and leave the place Re-joic-ing in the Lord.

D. S.—Go-ing a-way from glo-rious light, From par-don, life and God.

CHORUS.   *D. S.*

Going a-way unsaved to-night, A-way from redeem-ing blood;

Copyright, 1887, by D. B. Towner.

The Haven of Rest.

Dr H. L. Gilmour. Geo. D. Moore.

1. My soul, in sad exile, was out on life's sea, So burdened with sin, and distrest, Till I heard a sweet voice saying, My fetters fell off, and I anchored my soul; The haven of rest is my Lord.
2. I yielded myself to his tender embrace, And faith taking hold of the word, Of Jesus, who'll save whosoever will have A home in the "Haven of Rest!"
3. The song of my soul, since the Lord made me whole, Has been the OLD STORY so blest, Of Jesus, who'll save whosoever will have A home in the "Haven of Rest!"
4. How precious the thought that we all may recline, Like John the beloved and blest, On Jesus' strong arm, where no tempest can harm,—Secure in the "Haven of Rest!"
5. Oh, come to the Saviour, he patiently waits To save by his power divine; Come, anchor your soul in the haven of rest, And say, "my Beloved is mine."

D.S.—The tempest may sweep o'er the wild, stormy deep, In Jesus I'm safe evermore.

CHORUS.

I've anchored my soul in the haven of rest, I'll sail the wide seas no more,

Copyright, 1889, by John J. Hood.

180. Thou art Drifting.

FOR MALE VOICES.

P. B.   P. Bilhorn. By per.

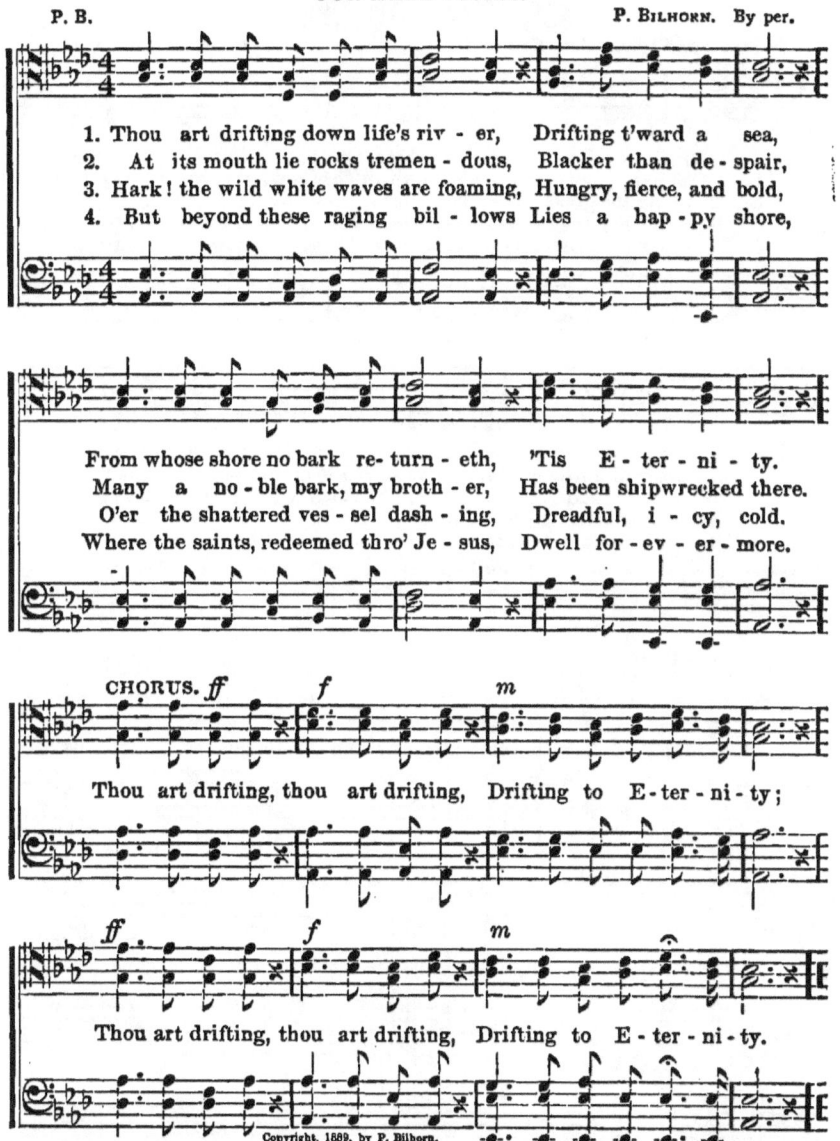

1. Thou art drifting down life's riv-er, Drifting t'ward a sea, From whose shore no bark re-turn-eth, 'Tis E-ter-ni-ty.
2. At its mouth lie rocks tremen-dous, Blacker than de-spair, Many a no-ble bark, my broth-er, Has been shipwrecked there.
3. Hark! the wild white waves are foaming, Hungry, fierce, and bold, O'er the shattered ves-sel dash-ing, Dreadful, i-cy, cold.
4. But beyond these raging bil-lows Lies a hap-py shore, Where the saints, redeemed thro' Je-sus, Dwell for-ev-er-more.

CHORUS.
Thou art drifting, thou art drifting, Drifting to E-ter-ni-ty;
Thou art drifting, thou art drifting, Drifting to E-ter-ni-ty.

Copyright, 1889, by P. Bilhorn.

5 O my friend, thy bark shall never
   Reach that happy shore
Till the Lord becomes your Pilot,
   He will guide thee o'er.

6 Call him with entreaty urgent,
   Call him near thy side,
Then o'er roughest, darkest billows,
   Safely thou shalt glide.

181. Oh, Happy Day!

Words adapted by Mrs. I. S. Kress.   Arr. by Jno. R. Sweney.

1. Oh, happy day that fixed my choice On thee, my Saviour and my God!
2. Oh, happy bond, that seals my vows To him who merits all my love!
3. 'Tis done, the great transaction's done; I am my Lord's, and he is mine;
4. Now rest, my long-di-vid-ed heart; Fixed on this blissful center, rest;
5. High heav'n, that heard the solemn vow, That vow renewed shall daily hear,

Well may this glowing heart rejoice, And tell its raptures all a-broad.
Let cheerful anthems fill his house, While to that sacred shrine I move.
He drew me, and I followed on, Charmed to confess the voice di-vine.
Nor ev-er from thy Lord depart, With him of ev-'ry good possessed.
Till in life's lat-est hour I bow, And bless in death a bond so dear.

REFRAIN.

He taught me how to watch and pray, and live re-joicing every day;

Oh, happy day, oh, happy day, When Jesus washed my sins a-way!

Oh, happy day, oh, happy day, When Jesus washed my sins a-way!

Copyright, 1892, by John J. Hood.

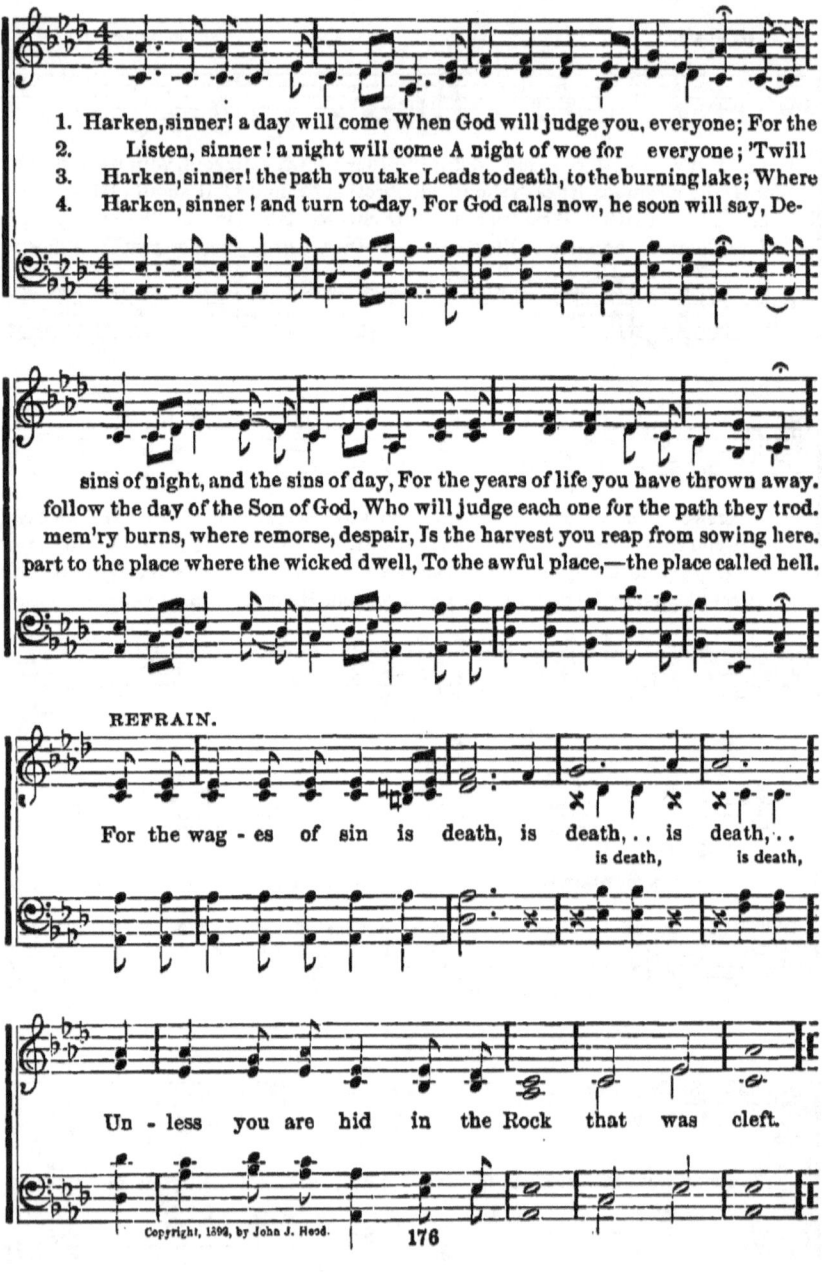

Come unto Me.

Wm. J. Kirkpatrick.

188. Will You be There?

Mrs. I. S. Kress.
Arr. by Jno. R. Sweney.

1. Beyond this life of hopes and fears, Beyond this world of griefs and tears, There is a region, a region fair, Oh, tell me, will you, will you be there? It knows no change and no decay, No night, but one un-ending day; It's glorious gates are closed to sin, Naught that defiles, can enter in To mar its grandeur, its beauty

2. Upon that bright eternal shore Earth's bitter curse is known no more, No pain, no grief, no sorrow nor care, Tell me, oh, tell me, will you be there? No drooping form, no tearful eye, No hoary head, no weary sigh, But joys which mortals may not know, Like a calm river ever flow; Promise me, O sinner, that you'll be

3. Our Saviour once as mortal child, As mortal man, by man reviled—There many glorious crowns doth wear; Promise the Master that you'll be there! While thousand thousands swell the strain Of glory to the Lamb once slain. Helped by the Holy Spirit's power, I will this day, this very hour—Turn from my sins unto Christ the

Copyright, 1892, by John J. Hood.

190. Waiting for the Harvest.

E. E. Hewitt. Wm. J. Kirkpatrick.

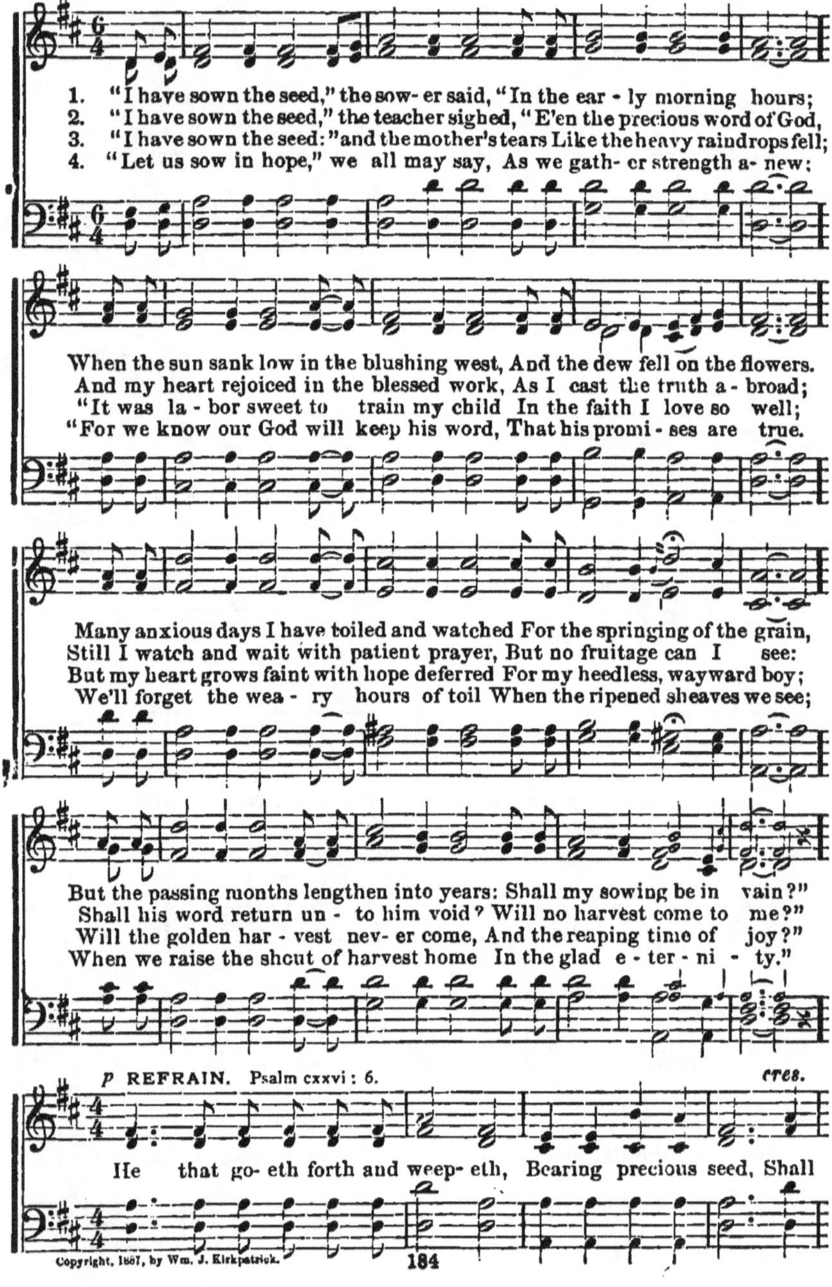

1. "I have sown the seed," the sow-er said, "In the ear-ly morning hours;
2. "I have sown the seed," the teacher sighed, "E'en the precious word of God,
3. "I have sown the seed:" and the mother's tears Like the heavy raindrops fell;
4. "Let us sow in hope," we all may say, As we gath-er strength a-new;

When the sun sank low in the blushing west, And the dew fell on the flowers.
And my heart rejoiced in the blessed work, As I cast the truth a-broad;
"It was la-bor sweet to train my child In the faith I love so well;
"For we know our God will keep his word, That his promi-ses are true.

Many anxious days I have toiled and watched For the springing of the grain,
Still I watch and wait with patient prayer, But no fruitage can I see:
But my heart grows faint with hope deferred For my heedless, wayward boy;
We'll forget the wea-ry hours of toil When the ripened sheaves we see;

But the passing months lengthen into years: Shall my sowing be in vain?"
Shall his word return un-to him void? Will no harvest come to me?"
Will the golden har-vest nev-er come, And the reaping time of joy?"
When we raise the shout of harvest home In the glad e-ter-ni-ty."

p REFRAIN. Psalm cxxvi: 6. *cres.*

He that go-eth forth and weep-eth, Bearing precious seed, Shall

Copyright, 1887, by Wm. J. Kirkpatrick.

184

194. His Yoke is Easy.

Ps. xxiii.   R. E. Hudson.

1. The Lord is my Shepherd, I shall not want, He maketh me down to lie In pastures green, He leadeth me The qui-et wa-ters by.
2. My soul crieth out: "restore me again, And give me the strength to take The narrow path of righteousness, E'en for his own name's sake."
3. Yea, tho' I should walk in the valley of death, Yet why should I fear from ill? For thou art with me, and thy rod And staff me comfort still.

CHORUS.

His yoke is eas-y, His burden is light, I've found it so, I've found it so; He lead-eth me, by day and by night, Where living waters flow.

195. Jesus, I my Cross have taken.

Tune on opposite page.

1 Jesus, I my cross have taken,
  All to leave and follow thee;
Naked, poor, despised, forsaken,
  Thou, from hence, my all shalt be:
Perish ev'ry fond ambition,
  All I've sought and hoped, and known;
Yet how rich is my condition,
  God and heaven are still my own!

2 Let the world despise and leave me,
  They have left my Saviour, too;
Human hearts and looks deceive me;
  Thou art not, like man, untrue;
And, while thou shalt smile upon me,
  God of wisdom, love, and might,
Foes may hate and friends may shun me;
  Show thy face, and all is bright.

3 Go, then, earthly fame and treasure!
  Come, disaster, scorn, and pain!
In thy service, pain is pleasure;
  With thy favor, loss is gain.
I have called thee, "Abba Father;"
  I have stayed my heart on thee;
Storms may howl, and clouds may gather,
  All must work for good to me.

196 Peace, Perfect Peace.

PAX TECUM, 10s., 2 lines.

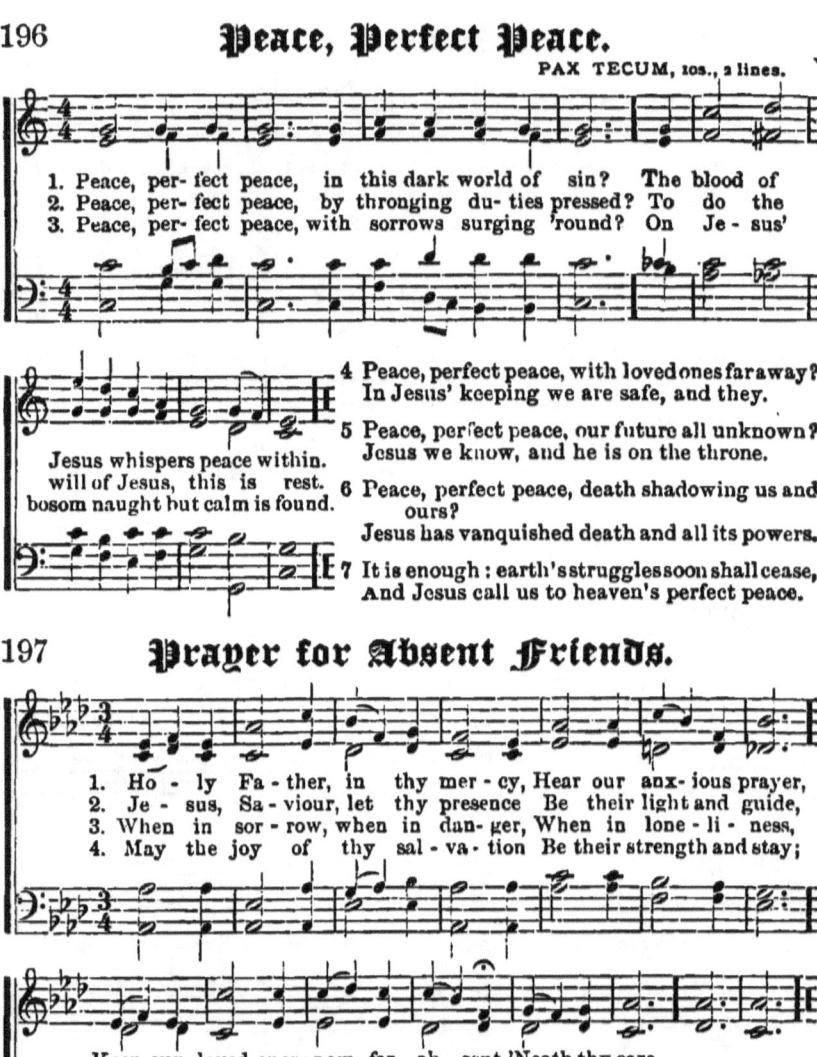

1. Peace, perfect peace, in this dark world of sin? The blood of Jesus whispers peace within.
2. Peace, perfect peace, by thronging duties pressed? To do the will of Jesus, this is rest.
3. Peace, perfect peace, with sorrows surging 'round? On Jesus' bosom naught but calm is found.
4 Peace, perfect peace, with loved ones far away? In Jesus' keeping we are safe, and they.
5 Peace, perfect peace, our future all unknown? Jesus we know, and he is on the throne.
6 Peace, perfect peace, death shadowing us and ours? Jesus has vanquished death and all its powers.
7 It is enough: earth's struggles soon shall cease, And Jesus call us to heaven's perfect peace.

197 Prayer for Absent Friends.

1. Holy Father, in thy mercy, Hear our anxious prayer, Keep our loved ones now far absent 'Neath thy care.
2. Jesus, Saviour, let thy presence Be their light and guide, Keep, oh, keep them in their weakness At thy side.
3. When in sorrow, when in danger, When in loneliness, In thy love look down and comfort Their distress.
4. May the joy of thy salvation Be their strength and stay; May they love, and may they praise thee Day by day.

A-men.

5 Holy Spirit, let thy teaching
  Sanctify their life,
Send thy grace that they may conquer
  In the strife.

6 Father, Son, and Holy Spirit,
  God the One in three, [them
Bless them, guide them, save them, keep
  Near to thee. Amen.

198.

SCOTCH MELODY.

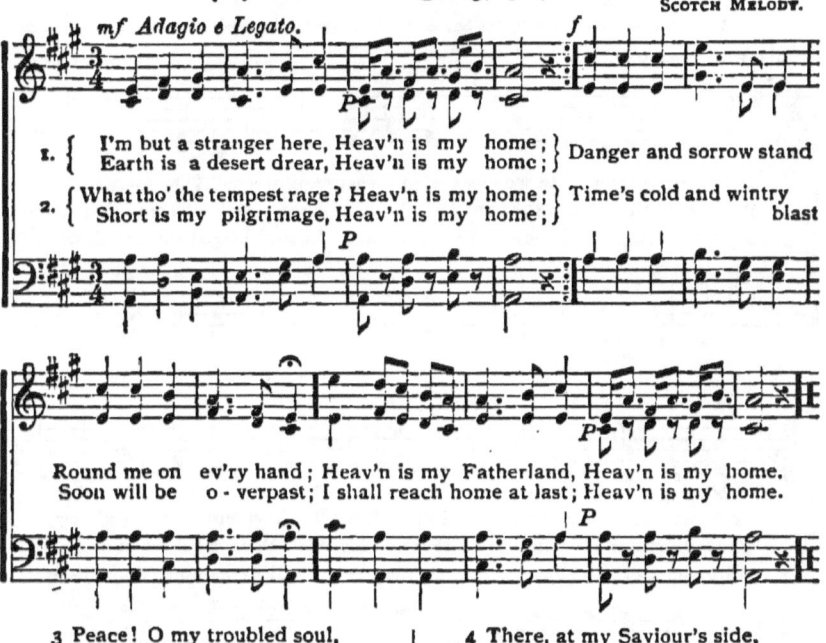

1. I'm but a stranger here, Heav'n is my home;
   Earth is a desert drear, Heav'n is my home;
   Danger and sorrow stand
   Round me on ev'ry hand; Heav'n is my Fatherland, Heav'n is my home.

2. What tho' the tempest rage? Heav'n is my home;
   Short is my pilgrimage, Heav'n is my home;
   Time's cold and wintry blast
   Soon will be o-verpast; I shall reach home at last; Heav'n is my home.

3 Peace! O my troubled soul,
  Heav'n is my home;
  I soon shall reach the goal;
  Heav'n is my home;
  Swiftly the race I'll run,
  Yield up my crown to none;
  Forward! the prize is won;
  Heav'n is my home.

4 There, at my Saviour's side,
  Heav'n is my home;
  I shall be glorified;
  Heav'n is my home;
  There are the good and blest,
  Those I loved most and best,
  There, too, I soon shall rest,
  Heav'n is my home.

199. Nearer, My God! to Thee.

1 Nearer, my God! to thee,
  Nearer to thee!
  E'en though it be a cross
  That raiseth me!
  Still all my song shall be,
  Nearer, my God! to thee,
  Nearer to thee!

2 Though like the wanderer,
  The sun gone down,
  Darkness be over me,
  My rest a stone,
  Yet in my dreams I'd be
  Nearer, my God! to thee,
  Nearer to thee!

3 There let the way appear,
  Steps unto heaven;
  All that thou sendest me,
  In mercy given;
  Angels to beckon me
  Nearer, my God! to thee,
  Nearer to thee!

4 Then, with my waking thoughts
  Bright with thy praise,
  Out of my stony griefs
  Bethel I'll raise;
  So by my woes to be
  Nearer, my God! to thee,
  Nearer to thee!

5 Or if, on joyful wing
  Cleaving the sky,
  Sun, moon and stars forgot,
  Upward I fly,
  Still all my song shall be,
  Nearer, my God! to thee,
  Nearer to thee!

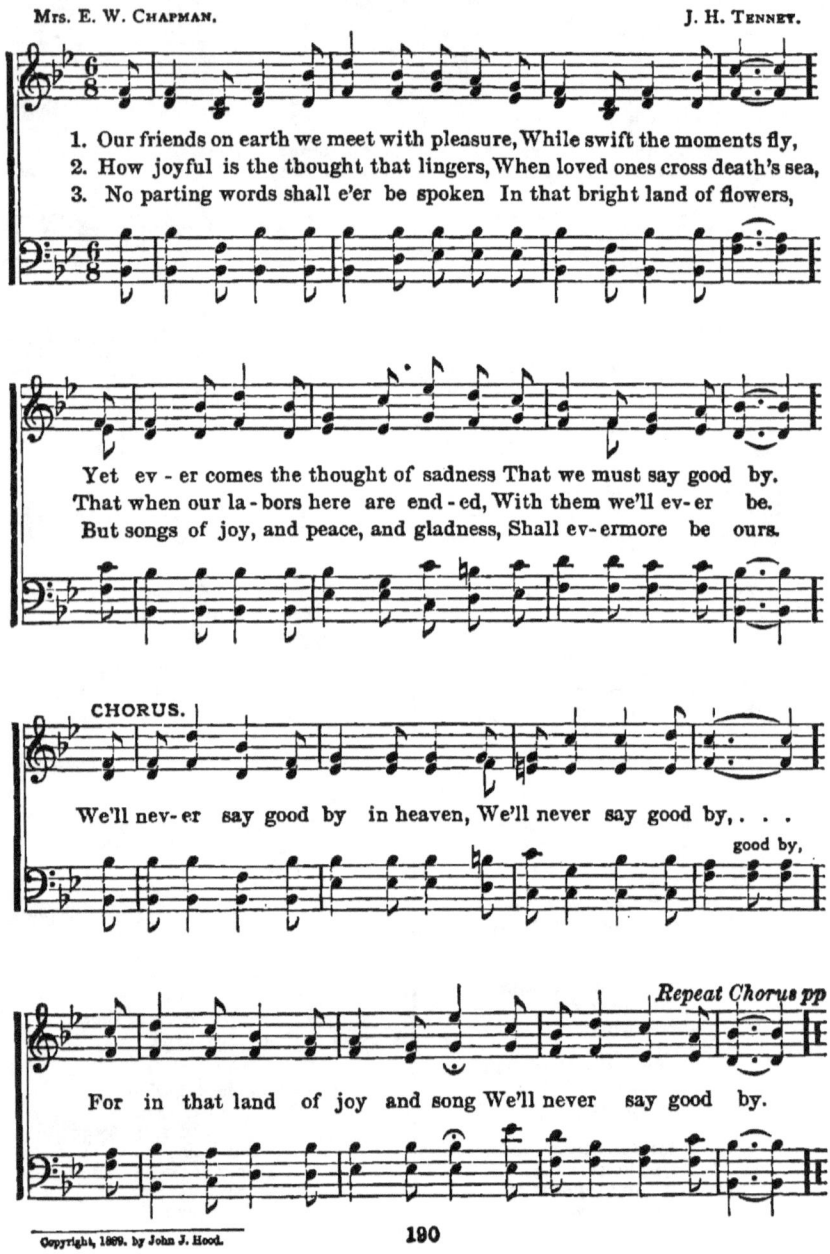

INDEX.

Titles in CAPITALS; First lines in Roman.

	HYMN.		HYMN.		HYMN.
ABIDING,	5	Down in the valley with.	53	I entered once a home	178
A little talk with Jesus,	131	DOXOLOGY,	164	I have a song I love to.	166
ALWAYS ABOUNDING,	8	Do you hear that gentle	129	I have found a balm for	55
ANCHORED ON THE	62	DRINKING AT THE LIV-	55	I have found a friend di-	142
And he journeyed with.	167			I have found a friend in	66
Are you drifting down	40	Each cooing dove and	75	I have found repose for.	146
Are you ready for the	6	ENTIRE CONSECRATION	109	I have sown the seed the	190
ARE YOU WASHED IN	125	EVERY DAY,	90	I hope to meet you all	35
A ruler once came to Je-	23			I'LL LIVE FOR HIM,	51
ARE YOU COMING.	126	Far out on the desolate.	19	I love my Saviour, his	4
Are you weary, are you.	28	FED UPON THE FINEST	191	I'm but a stranger here,.	198
A SHELTER IN THE	133	FILL ME NOW,	25	In the Christian's home.	152
A SINNER LIKE ME,	59	FOLLOW ON,	53	IN THE MORNING,.	16
AT THE CROSS,	52	Friends of yore have	15	In the shadow of his	54
AT THE CROSS I'LL A-	88			In thy cleft, O Rock of.	1
AT THE FOUNTAIN,	154	GATHERING HOME,	171	Into his image to grow,.	96
AT THE GOLDEN LAND-	15	GIVE ME JESUS,	37	In vain in high and holy	18
At the sounding of the.	68	GLORIOUS FOUNTAIN,	73	I praise the Lord that	97
Awake, awake, O Zion,.	118	Glory be to the Father,	164	Is it well with your soul.	182
Awake, sinful heart, the	186	GLORY TO GOD, HAL-	128	IS MY NAME WRITTEN.	32
		Glory to Jesus who died	46	IS NOT THIS THE LAND	31
Be earnest, my brothers,	8	God be with you till we.	64	Is there any one here	94
BEHOLD THE BRIDE-	6	God loved the world so	42	IS YOUR LAMP BURNING	33
BEHOLD, THE FIELDS	114	GOING AWAY UNSAVED	177	IT REACHES ME,	102
Beyond this life of hopes	188	Great is the Lord, who.	78	I want to be a worker	20
Blessed assurance, Jesus	30			I was once far away	59
Blessed be the fountain.	36	HAPPY LAND,	156	I WILL SHOUT HIS	100
Blessed Saviour, my sal-	115	HAPPY TIDINGS,	60	I WILL TRUST IN THEE	115
BRINGING IN THE.	104	HEAR AND ANSWER	101		
Brother for Christ's	21	Hearken, sinner! a day	183	Jesus, I come to thee,	91
BUT THE LORD IS	167	HEAVEN IS MY HOME,	198	JESUS IS GOOD TO ME,	4
BY THE GRACE OF GOD	58	Hark, hark, my soul, an-	113	JESUS IS PASSING BY,	184
		Hark the song of holy	193	JESUS IS STRONG TO DE-	174
Called to the feast by	110	HARVEST TIME,	169	Jesus, Lover of my soul	84
CALVARY,	70	Have you been to Jesus	125	Jesus, my Lord, to thee.	79
Cast thy bread upon the	12	Hear the footsteps of Je-	72	Jesus my Saviour to	93
CAST THY BURDEN ON.	17	HE CAME TO SAVE ME,.	112	JESUS OF NAZARETH	61
CHRIST AROSE,	98	HE COMES,	118	JESUS SAVES,.	85
CHRIST IS ALL,	178	HE IS CALLING,	161	Jesus, Saviour, pilot me,	170
COME AND SEE,	111	HELP JUST A LITTLE,	21	Jesus, the rock on which	117
Come, contrite one, and	184	Here in thy name we	123	Jesus when he left the	137
Come, every soul by sin.	147	HE SAVES,	29	JESUS WILL MEET YOU.	121
Come, humble sinner, in	147	HE WILL GATHER THE	176	JOY IN ZION,	38
Come, sinners, to the	122	HIDE THOU ME,	1	Just as I am, without	79
Come to Calv'ry's mount	121	HIDING IN THEE,.	80		
COME TO JESUS,	147	HIS YOKE IS EASY,	194	KEEP STEP EVER,.	95
Come unto me, all ye	185	Holy Father in thy mer-	197		
Come, ye disconsolate,	153	Holy, holy, holy, Lord	143	Leading souls to Jesus	43
COMING TO-DAY,	56	HOME AT LAST,	193	LEAD ME, SAVIOUR,	65
CONSECRATION,	77	Hover o'er me, Holy	25	LEANING ON JESUS,	140
CLEANSING WAVE,	163	How firm a foundation,.	144	LET HIM IN,	148
CLINGING TO THE.	106	Hungry, Lord, for thy	191	Let the children of Zion	38
CROWN HIM,.	159			Light after darkness,	41
		I am coming to the cross	151	LITTLE ONES LIKE ME,.	137
Dark are the waters be-.	175	I am dwelling on the	31	Look up! behold, the	114
DO SOMETHING,	120	I am praying, blessed	101	Look, ye saints, the sight	159

TEMPLE SONGS.

Lord, I care not for	32	REDEEMED, PRAISE	145	Though there may be	90
Lord Jesus, I long to be	150	Repeat the story o'er	11	Tho' your sins be as	83
Low in the grave he lay,	98	REST FOR THE WEARY,	152	Through the gates of	58
		Resting in the love of	62	Tidings, happy tidings,	60
MARCHING ON,	45	Rise up, and hasten! my	67	'Tis the blessed hour of.	47
MEET IN THE MORNING	116	Rouse, ye saints, the	187	To thy cross, dear Christ	69
MEET ME THERE,.	130			Touch and cleanse me,	138
MEMORIES OF GALILEE	75	Saviour, blessed Saviour	105	TRIUMPH BY AND BY,	124
'Mid scenes of confusion	27	Saviour, lead me, lest I.	65	TRUSTING IN THE	146
More about Jesus would	173	SAVIOUR, PILOT ME,	170	Trustingly, trustingly,	77
MORE FAITH IN JESUS,	39	SAY, ARE YOU READY!.	7	Trying to walk in the	34
My body, soul, and spirit	77	Say, is your lamp burn-.	33		
My brother we are trav-	114	SEEKING FOR ME,.	93	Up to the bountiful Giv-	171
My faith looks up to	160	SEEKING TO SAVE,	87	Use me, O my gracious.	127
My Father is rich in	57	Should the death angel.	7		
My Jesus, I love thee,	149	SHOWERS OF BLESSING,	123	WAITING FOR THE	190
My life, my love I give-.	51	SINCE I HAVE BEEN	166	Walk in the light the	99
MY SHEPHERD,	136	Sing glory to God in the	29	We are marching on-	116
My soul, be on thy guard	82	Some go away from the.	177	We are never, never	128
My soul for light and	5	SOME SWEET DAY,	26	We are pilgrims looking	16
My soul in sad exile	179	Sometimes the sky is	14	Weary pilgrim on life's	17
		So near the door, and	189	Weary with walking a-.	140
Nearer, my God! to thee	199	Sound the battle-cry,	22	We have heard a joyful.	85
NEVER ALONE,	19	Sowing in the morning,.	104	We know not our path	119
NOTHING BUT THE	74	Speak to me, Jesus,	48	WE'LL WORK TILL JE-	155
		STEPPING IN THE..	34	WE'LL NEVER SAY	200
Of him who did salva-	154	Stepping-stones to Jesus	165	We're traveling home to	157
O happy day! what a	145	SWEET HOME,	27	We shall have a new	135
Oh, happy day that	181	SWEET PEACE, THE	81	We shall reach the river	26
Oh, bliss of the purified	49			WHAT A GATHERING	68
Oh, I often sit and pon-.	50	TAKE ME AS I AM,	79	What can wash away my	74
Oh, now I see the.	163	Take my life and let it.	109	What means this eager,.	61
OH, SING OF HIS	49	TELL IT TO JESUS,	28	WHAT'S THE NEWS,	63
Oh, this uttermost salva-	102	Tell me the story of Je-	107	WHAT TIME I AM A-	14
OH! 'TIS GLORY IN MY	69	Tenderly the Shepherd,	87	What will you do with	76
Oh, to have the mind of	108	THAT GENTLE WHIS-	129	Whene'er we meet we	63
O Jesus, Lord, thy dy-.	52	THE CHILD OF A KING	57	When I'm happy hear	37
O Jesus, Saviour, I long	88	THE FIRM FOUNDATION	144	When in the tempest	174
O land of rest, for thee.	155	THE FUTURE,	50	When Jesus laid his	112
O, my heart is full of	106	THE GOLDEN KEY,	162	When Jesus shall gather	176
On Calvary's brow my	70	The Great Physician,	82	When my Saviour I	86
One more day it's twi-	9	THE HALF WAS NEVER	11	WHEN THE KING,	110
On Jordan's stormy	103	THE HAVEN OF REST,	179	When we enter the por-.	89
On let us go where the	132	THE LAND JUST ACROSS	103	While Jesus whispers to	158
Only a beam of sunshine	134	THE LILY OF THE VAL-	66	While struggling through	39
On the happy, golden	130	The Lord is my	136, 194	WHITER THAN SNOW,.	150
O prodigal, don't stay a-	44	The Lord's our Rock, in	133	WHOSOEVER,	97
O safe to the Rock that.	80	THE MIND OF JESUS,	108	WHY DON'T YOU COME	172
O, think of a home over	10	The morning light is	139	Why do you wait, dear.	92
Our friends on earth we.	200	THE NEW NAME,	135	WILL YOU BE THERE?.	188
Out on the desert, look-.	56	THE NEW SONG,	24	WILL YOU GO?	114, 157
OVER JORDAN,	71	THE NUMBERLESS HOST	89	WILT THOU BE MADE.	72
OVER THERE,	10	The prize is set before us	124	With his dear and loving	71
OVER THE TIDE,	175	There are songs of joy	24	With our colors waving.	45
O ye wand'rers, come to	172	There comes to my	81	WONDERFUL LOVE OF.	18
		There is a fountain	73	WON'T YOU LOVE MY	142
Peace, perfect peace, in.	196	There is a happy land,	156	Would you gain the best	95
PRAISE AND MAGNIFY.	78	There is pardon sweet	141		
Praise to thee, Mighty	13	There's a stranger at the	148	YE MUST BE BORN A-	23
PRAYER FOR ABSENT	197	There's a wideness in	161	You ask what makes	100
Prayer is the key for the	162	The seed I have scat-	169	You have heard the gos-	126
		THE VERY SAME JESUS,	122	You're longing to work.	120
Redeemed, how I love	111	Thou art drifting down.	180		

www.ingramcontent.com/pod-product-compliance
Lightning Source LLC
Chambersburg PA
CBHW020239170426
43202CB00008B/148